T0208437

STAND TO: FINDING MASCULINE COURAGE
IN A STAND DOWN WORLD
SHAWN BROWER

The world says we need less masculinity, that it's in the nature of men to be toxic to those around them. Shawn Brower thinks that the world is suffering from a lack of courageous men who know who they are, whose they are, and what they are for. I'm with Shawn, and not only because the Bible teaches what Shawn so clearly describes in Stand To. For years, Shawn has been training boys to be men, and this book proves he's the kind of guide we need right now."
John Stonestreet,
President of the Colson Center for Christian Worldview and host of BreakPoint

We now live in a country where masculinity is under attack.... While "toxic masculinity" has always existed, we must never allow Christ centered masculinity to be removed from society. It's time for men of God to stand up not down. Shawn Brower points to God's standard of masculinity and invites men to embrace who God designed us to be.
Rick Burgess,
Co-Host of the Rick and Bubba Show and Director of TheManChurch.com

Men who would "stand up for Christ" and "stand firm in Christ" would benefit from being saturated in Dr. Brower's volume Stand To – a weighty yet engaging exposition of Christ- exalting Biblical masculinity. Enjoy and profit!
Harry L. Reeder, III
Senior Pastor, Briarwood Presbyterian Church

I have been told by a much wiser man than myself that I am among the most frightened men he had ever met. I heard those words almost 30 years ago as he lovingly confronted me. I have been in pursuit of help and insight ever since I was told this in order to face this tragic mark of my broken life with the grace of God in the Gospel. Shawn and Josh Brower have placed a glorious help in my hands. This book unmasked my self-absorption and my Jesus-minimization. Having shown me myself, it then called me and equipped me to "Stand To" because of my King, by the grace of my King, for the glory of my King. I am a thankful debtor to the Browers for this help. Frightened like me? I believe you will find significant help and insight right here.
Joseph V. Novenson
Pastor to Senior Adults
Lookout Mountain Presbyterian Church

"This book helps men, young or old, to courageously pursue, accept, and act on God's masculine design, to image Jesus who, humbly and yet courageously, embraced the cross so others might live. A must read book for every man."
Mitch Temple
Executive Director / CoFounder - The Fatherhood CoMission

STAND TO

*Finding Masculine Courage in a
Stand Down World*

SHAWN BROWER

with *Josh Brower*

WESTBOW
PRESS®
A DIVISION OF THOMAS NELSON
& ZONDERVAN

WestBow Press books may be ordered through booksellers or by contacting:

WestBow Press
A Division of Thomas Nelson & Zondervan
1663 Liberty Drive
Bloomington, IN 47403
www.westbowpress.com
844-714-3454

Cover Design: Bryan White

ISBN: 978-1-6642-1734-8 (sc)
ISBN: 978-1-6642-1735-5 (hc)
ISBN: 978-1-6642-1733-1 (e)

Library of Congress Control Number: 2020925415

Print information available on the last page.

WestBow Press rev. date: 2/2/2021

To my father

Through a lifetime in the ministry to Jesus Christ, over fifty years
of faithful marriage to my incredible mother, and a model of true
godly manhood to my three sons and me, I am eternally grateful
for the Christlike example he set and lived. *Stand To* sums up his
resolve, consistency, and persistence to live a life that has counted
and will echo through eternity and around the throne of God!

Special Thanks

Proverbs 18:22 says that *"He who finds a wife finds a good thing and obtains favor from the Lord."* (ESV)

I was undeservedly blessed beyond measure and comprehension nearly 28 years ago when my wife and best friend said, "I DO!"

Through every pursuit, change, challenge, and opportunity, the constant through it all was the abiding love, enduring faithfulness, and unconditional support of my wife, Shawn (same name).

This most recent project of writing this book was no exception. Her feedback, encouragement, and editing deserves rightful recognition and appreciation.

Thank you Shawn - you truly are the BEST and I love you!

Contents

FOREWORD

We all want the same things, don't we? We want something to live for. We want to feel like what we do is going somewhere. We want to feel like our lives really matter. You feel it deeply, don't you? If so, then you have found your way to exactly the right book at exactly the right moment.

Don't you just love rubbing shoulders with an excited, passionate man who really knows what he's doing? Shawn Brower is such a man. I first met Shawn twenty-two years ago when he was coaching our son in soccer. From the first day I saw him in action, I knew Shawn was destined for greatness.

And now you're about to see for yourself why I would follow him into battle, with no questions asked. He's led his schools to five state men's soccer championships. He's been selected national Coach of the Year three times! This man has guts. He's humble, but he doesn't pull punches. And he's highly contagious!

Stand To stirred something deep inside me. It has grit. The appeal is not to be a soft, passive, meek-and-mild kind of guy. But rather, like Jesus, it's to grab hold of your courage and face the juggernaut of our current cultural climate head-on. I felt fresh courage coursing through my veins as I read Shawn's stories.

I get a heroic vibe every time I read a few pages of this book. But far from a hoorah, suck-it-up, you-can-do-it approach, Brower makes his appeal on the basis of how we can anchor ourselves in the life and teachings of Jesus Christ.

In ancient Greece when Isocrates spoke, the people said, "How well he speaks." But when Demosthenes spoke, the people said, "Let's march against Philip!" This is that kind of book. But it's not just a call to action. Brower will lead you through a series of Courage Challenges that will help get you where you want to go.

Stand To is going to light your hair on fire. This incredibly interesting and highly readable book is destined to reach a whole new generation of men who want their lives to count and make a difference.

Patrick Morley, PhD
Founder, Man in the Mirror
Author of *The Man in the Mirror* and twenty other books

WHERE ARE ALL THE MEN?

*Men of Issachar, who had understanding of the
times, to know what Israel ought to do.*
—1 CHRONICLES 12:32 (ESV)

In 2012 I wrote the book, *We Became Men: The Journey into Manhood*. At that time, the impetus and my intent in writing that book stemmed from watching young men flounder in their attempt to navigate the culture in which they were growing up. As I looked around, I saw young men, my three sons included, growing up in a world where boyhood and adulthood were ill-defined and clear rites of passage were becoming close to nonexistent. In fact, new words and ideas were emerging in an attempt to make sense of the quandary our male population seemed mired in as they struggled to understand masculine identity and purpose for existence. The teen years and transition to adult years had quickly become blurred and extended. The new term *adultolescent* emerged to define or describe this new generation.

By definition, *adultolescent* means "a young adult or middle-aged person who has interests, traits, etc., that are usually associated with teenagers."[1]

Many of these men, now in their late twenties and early thirties, were paralyzed by indecision and a gross lack of understanding of what it means to be a man as they pursued time-consuming, mind-numbing, heart-destroying patterns, unaware of the ramifications for these actions.

While such actions persisted, I saw an incredible opportunity all around me with young men so capable and able to assume the mantle of manhood, if only guidance and direction were offered, received, and applied. I saw untapped potential just waiting to be revealed and released if they could just be pulled away from the joystick lulling them into a state of apathy, stupor, and false adventure. So as a man of God, a father of three sons, and one who daily works with teenage guys, wishing they had more of an understanding of manhood, I intended to provide a trail map for this journey toward manhood as manhood, masculinity, and gender identity continue to be redefined and realigned with an agenda not in accordance with God's Word and His moral standard. Guys need to know what they will encounter on their journey and how to stand against a liberal agenda and secular ideology that will cause them to be thought of as intolerant and will likely lead to antagonistic harassment and religious liberty persecution. This is why we must take encouragement from the truth of God's Word and His sovereignty over all the affairs of our lives, for there is nothing of this world that exceeds His providential plan.

Since 2012 when *We Became Men* was released, my writing has now taken a distinct shift and a more narrowed focus as the liberal agenda seeks to not just redefine but sabotage the male gender at the earliest age possible. In fact, even feminist Camille Paglia saw this coming years ago as she stated in a *Wall Street Journal* article, "Primary-school education is a crock. They're making a toxic environment for boys. It's oppressive to anyone with physical energy, especially boys. Primary education does everything in its power to turn boys into neuters … and the same thing happens all the way to college. This PC gender politics thing—the way gender is being taught in the universities—is a very anti-male way. It is all about neutralization of maleness." She concludes, "What you're seeing is how a civilization commits suicide."[2]

It is time to wake up, men! We cannot acquiesce to the intentional movement of emasculating our gender. It might be easy to assign blame to the culture or some external group, but the reality is that we too are to blame for allowing ourselves to buy into the redefinition of our masculinity, to be suckered into marketing ploys playing on our fascinations and desires that render us passive, apathetic, ineffective, and stuck in neutral.

Too hard a statement? Judge for yourself. The video game revenue in 2018 reached a new peak of $43.8 billion, up 18 percent from previous years.[3] As the *NY Post* cited in an article entitled "We're Losing a Whole Generation of Young Men to Video Games,"

> the problem is that for many young men, video games have become a substitute for living. They're so addictive and soul-consuming that they're unlike other leisure activities. Every hour spent on "Ghost Recon" or "Grand Theft Auto V" is an hour that could have been spent more productively.[4]

In an article in *Forbes* from March 2019, it stated that the average gamer spends over eight hours a week gaming and that "the largest increase of gaming was from the 26–35 age group with about a 26% increase."[5]

While these increasing numbers are staggering, they certainly are rivaled by another soul-deteriorating, heartbreaking, addictive entrapment with the rapid rise and accessibility of pornography. Check out these research facts provided by Covenant Eyes:

- 51 percent of male students first viewed porn before their teenage years.
- Their first exposure to pornography was twelve years old, on average.

- 71 percent say they hide this online behavior from their parents.[6]

Yet should we be surprised? Fight the New Drug website offers the following statistics about pornography:

- "Porn is a global, estimated $97 billion industry, with about $12 billion of that coming from the U.S.
- In 2018 alone, more than 5,517,000,000 hours of porn were consumed on the world's largest porn site."[7] Covenant Eyes offers the damaging effects of this pornography on the lives and relationships of men:
  - "1 in 5 youth pastors and 1 in 7 senior pastors use porn on a regular basis and are currently struggling. That's more than 50,000 U.S. church leaders.
  - 68% of divorce cases involved one party meeting a new lover over the Internet.
  - 56% involved one party having 'an obsessive interest in pornographic websites.'
  - 70% of wives of sex addicts could be diagnosed with PTSD."[8]

Not only is there a time and relationship cost to the lives of men for the amount of time spent gaming and viewing pornography, but we also are seeing a loss of productive living. The *NY Post* reports, "Video-game addicts are engaged in a mass retreat from life. Men aged 21 to 30 worked 12 percent fewer hours in 2015 than in 2000. The percent of young men who worked zero weeks over the course of a year doubled in that period, to an alarming 15 percent."[9]

It is also interesting that according to the US Census Bureau, as of 2017, nearly one in five men aged twenty-five to thirty-four lived in their parents' homes. In raw-number terms, 4.3 million men twenty-five to thirty-four are living with their parents. That population is approximately the size of the entire adult and child population of Arizona. In 2016, the Pew Research Center noted that more young adults ages eighteen to thirty-four were living with their parents than with a spouse or partner. This is the first time that's happened in at least 130 years.[10]

Yet this is bigger than wasting hours gaming and hours engrossed in pornography, which sadly leads to a less productive citizen in society. A systemic problem today continues to get worse. In just a few short years since I wrote *We Became Men*, the landscape around us has so quickly pivoted before our very eyes, and the footing below our feet is shifting like never before in history. As identity exploration and self-discovery distract and sidetrack guys from good movement forward, the confusion of identity and lack of understanding of a man's purpose and direction in life continue to plummet at a remarkable rate.

With the June 26, 2015, *Obergefell v. Hodges* Supreme Court opinion regarding same-sex marriage, it not only redefined marriage between a man and a woman for the first time in history but accelerated, like never before, the acceptance of the redefinition of our God-ordained gender assignments to be whatever one chooses. Society now claims there are over sixty different genders by which people can identify.

Should we be surprised with the June 15, 2020, Supreme Court ruling, *Bostock v. Clayton County,* where the decision ruled that Title VII of the 1964 Civil Rights Act, which prohibited discrimination in employment on the basis of sex (male and female), should now also refer to and include discrimination based on sexual orientation and gender identity?

While I am not surprised at this, I was astounded that it happened only five years after, almost to the day, the *Obergefell v. Hodges* Supreme Court opinion. In response to the SCOTUS ruling, John Stonestreet, president of the Colson Center, writes,

> The consequences of yesterday's ruling will be significant. It is, to be clear, a broad ruling masquerading as a narrow one. This is more likely the beginning of a national SOGI law, in which sexual orientation and gender identity are equated with race and protections are extended and applied to other

areas of the Civil Rights Act, including those that govern housing and education.[11]

Stand To is a sequel to *We Became Men*. This book is now calling on men to be informed and equipped to step out from the tree line and into the open fields where, yes, we are more exposed, are easy targets, and will come under attack, but where we are also focused, ready, and willing to actively engage in the good endeavor of courageously living from our masculine design given to us by our Creator. In the final chapter of *We Became Men*, "Preparing for the Next Expedition," my challenge to guys was threefold:

- Understand you have much to offer the people around you
- Know you will grow in your masculine design as you stick to the right path, even when it is difficult
- Trust that God will prepare and equip you for what lies before you

That time is now! *We Became Men* was all about a mentoring relationship in one's journey toward manhood. However, the next challenge, or expedition, is now before you! As Moses influenced Joshua, Elijah affected Elisha, and Paul instructed Timothy, the time came when the mentor stepped aside and the one who was in training grew up, stepped up, and assumed his position. Yet the life and words of these mentors made a lasting impact on the one following behind as their life began to mirror that of their mentor in both words and deeds.

So as it did for these men, the pursuit of knowledge and truth must continue. The ultimate goal, however, is not just for our own benefit but to act in a way that positively affects and serves those in our area of influence. You might quickly conclude that you are not ready for this. That is fine. Moses, Elijah, and Paul all had questions or doubts as to their preparedness. If you wait until you believe you are ready, you will never move forward. You will be frozen by fear, insecurity, and doubt. Yet move you must, even in that state of fear, insecurity, and doubt, for it is through such difficult steps that courage is forged!

To refuse to step forward is evidence that you are only looking to your own strength. In reality, apart from God, you can do nothing. I am not suggesting that you suddenly become something you are not. Rather I am challenging you to simply live out of your God-designed maleness, trusting that, as God has designed you, He too will equip you for the good works in which He wants you to engage.

So what exactly is that? How is that defined, and who defines it for us? In a narcissistic, secular humanistic world, who answers that question for us is very important. Let's dig in here a bit.

There is no doubt that it is helpful to understand who is lining up on the other side of the ball, so to speak. To understand the posture and position of the culture we live in will be helpful as we navigate forward.

- We must realize that the prevailing culture wishes for us to be desensitized as agenda after agenda after agenda is pushed and promoted toward and against us. What was for shock value even ten or five years ago no longer is very shocking. What was thought forbidden and unacceptable now quickly has become the accepted new norm as we grow increasingly numb to it. We see this desensitization even back in the time of the prophet Jeremiah. Jeremiah 6:15 says, "Were they ashamed when they committed abomination? No, they were not at all ashamed; they did not know how to blush" (ESV).
- We must realize that competing forces utilize culture jamming to disrupt or subvert media and mainstream institutions, oftentimes through corporate advertising. While these forces attempt to foster progressive change, the ideologies now proposed could possibly be even worse as they seek to redirect the thinking of people at large.
- We must understand that the reality is that culture makers and shapers seek conversions to what they are attempting to portray as the popular thinking or ideal of the day. We can't be naïve that the messaging that is so loud today is not just noise. Rather it intends to convert from and subvert the Judeo-Christian way of thinking and living.

So what happens is that culture gives us what we assume are the default settings that we should be operating in as the prevailing thought and action of the day establishes the norm. It is almost like whoever has the loudest voice wins. In *The Social Animal*, David Brooks explains, "We wander across an environment of people and possibilities. As we wander, the mind makes a near-infinite number of value judgments which accumulate to formulate goals, ambitions, dreams, desires, and ways of doing things."[12] In other words, our culture will communicate and orient how we think, live, and decide … if we let them!

So as books are written, movies are created, visual stories are drawn, and billboard space is occupied, we find that, cumulatively, culture calls us to essentially worship and be worshippers of certain kinds of things. And they will define what those things are that we ought to be worshipping.

But what if in our consuming, copying, criticizing, or even condemning of what culture has to offer and say, we are missing the very essence of what we are called to be doing as people (men) made in the image of God? Aren't we to be caught up into a far grander narrative known as God's redemptive story?

I get it. It is easy to be overwhelmed and think the sky is falling. But we must remember that the Ancient of Days sits on His throne as He always has and always will and He beckons or invites us into this wonderful story where we might offer our very best in helping to shape the world where we are and as we were created and designed to do way back in the garden of Eden!

How do we know what that looks like? The answer does not lie in the culture around us. Rather we are blessed to have God's Word to know what is true, right, and good as our compass to guide us as we courageously embrace and boldly live out of our masculine design for the glory of God and the good of others! Stand to, men! For the alternative of standing down is not an option!

***

CHAPTER ONE

A LOOK UNDER THE HOOD

Do nothing from selfish ambition or conceit, but in humility count others more significant than yourself.
—PHILIPPIANS 2:3 (ESV)

Pride must die in you, or nothing of heaven can live in you.
—ANDREW MURRAY[13]

I'm Not the Problem Here!

We all need a point of reference, a point man upon whom we can emulate our lives. At first glance, Peter seems to be that guy. After all, Peter was a man's man. He was all about taking action and a stand and not sitting around and wasting time. Instead he was jumping into the fray and making things happen. Remember when Jesus was walking on the water toward the disciples' boat in a storm? What did Peter do? He got out of the boat and started walking on the water toward Jesus. When Judas betrayed Jesus and the soldiers and high priest came to take away Jesus, what did Peter do? He whipped out his sword and hacked off the high priest's ear! We would love to see that quick defense of Jesus and the heady action of Peter in any movie. Peter was an all-in kind of guy!

But wait, there was that defining moment recorded over 2,000 years ago when Peter, the other disciples, and Jesus are in a serious conversation about loyalty to Jesus as His moment of crucifixion is approaching. The dialogue goes like this:

> Then Jesus told them, "This very night you will all fall away on account of me, for it is written: 'I will strike the shepherd and the sheep of the flock will be scattered.' But after I have risen, I will go ahead of you into Galilee."
>
> Peter replied, "Even if all fall away on account of you, I never will."
>
> "Truly I tell you," Jesus answered, "this very night, before the rooster crows, you will disown me three times."
>
> But Peter declared, "Even if I have to die with you, I will never disown you." And all the other disciples said the same. (Matthew 26:31–35 NIV)

Whoa! What just happened there? Peter is told he is going to deny Jesus, and then Peter, without thinking, rushes headlong into a response of resolve, "I will never disown you." He is essentially saying, "You are wrong, Jesus! I would never do that!" He probably didn't even slow down enough to think that he was able to tell Jesus he had this all backward! Of course we know exactly what happened. Peter not only denied Jesus, he emphatically denied Him to the point of cursing out the accuser who was connecting him to Jesus!

Here is a guy who had been with Jesus every step of His ministry and was pledging his undying loyalty to Jesus. In fact, he separated himself as the elite loyalist to Jesus as he says, "Even if everyone falls away, I will never disown you!" How confident and self-assured Peter was that he had the situation all under control, yet in a moment he denied his King and Lord!

Before we hammer down on Peter, we have to ask ourselves if we are really all that different? How many times do we find ourselves thinking or even saying "I got this" or "I'm good"? Or do we, like Peter, just blurt out the first unmeasured thing that comes to mind? How should we respond in such weighty situations? Would we dare say that we all have some Peter in us? While not proud of it, we have more Peter in us than we would like to admit!

Broken Down

In the wake of the horrific killings of Black men Ahmaud Arbery and George Floyd at the hands of White men during the early summer of 2020, we saw our nation reeling as citizens weighed in on these gross injustices. Everyone had an immediate reaction as to what should have been done and who was to blame. People tried to figure out what the core issues were and are, how deeply embedded they are in our country's culture, and what the next right steps for immediate change needed to be. Sides were taken, and lines were quickly drawn as politics, race, government, economics, and everything in between were drawn into the unavoidable conflict our country was thrown into.

In the ensuing days, people were killed, cars and buildings were set on fire, people lost jobs, looters caused mayhem and violence, the coronavirus pandemic spread further as crowds gathered, and the unrest rivaled that of the post-Vietnam 1960s.

Many story lines emerged from this great conflict, but one in particular caught my attention. Future NFL Hall of Famer and New Orleans Saints quarterback, Drew Brees, made comments about his position on the American flag and how he would never support anyone disrespecting the flag for what it stood for to him.

Regardless of what one might think of his position of the American flag, most would conclude that the timing of his statement was poor. However, what followed was even more surprising than the visceral response he received from fans, teammates, and other professional athletes. Instead of doubling down and trying to explain his position, Drew Brees issued the following statement,

> I would like to apologize to my friends, teammates, the City of New Orleans, the black community, NFL community and anyone I hurt with my comments yesterday. In speaking with some of you, it breaks my heart to know the pain I have caused. In an attempt to talk about respect, unity, and solidarity centered around the American flag and the national anthem, I made comments that were insensitive and completely missed the mark on the issues we are facing right now as a country. They lacked awareness and any type of compassion or empathy. Instead, those words have become divisive and hurtful and have misled people into believing that somehow I am an enemy. This could not be further from the truth, and is not an accurate reflection of my heart or my character...I recognize that I am part of the solution and can be a leader for the black community in this movement. I will never know what it's like to be a black man or raise black children in America but I will work every day to put myself in those shoes and fight for what is right. I have ALWAYS been an ally, never an enemy. I am sick about the way my comments were perceived yesterday, but I take full responsibility and accountability. I recognize that I should do less talking and more listening ... and when the black community is talking about their pain, we all need to listen. For that, I am very sorry and I ask your forgiveness.[14]

Notice how Drew Brees begins by stating he wishes to apologize and that he is taking full responsibility and accountability and acknowledges he should do less talking and more listening. Then he ends by asking for forgiveness.

Whoa! What a response! In all the madness and mayhem, there was a response of humility and grace. At the same time, he did not compromise on his personal belief to stand for the American flag. He said, "I'll always stand for the flag because of what it means to me and to honor all those who served and died for our country, and all those who have struggled to move this country forward."[15] Notice how he humbly acknowledged that his comments were ill timed and not sensitive to the cultural moment, and yet he did not compromise his personal belief regarding the American flag. This is a commendable balance for sure.

Lifting the Hood

In most men's lives, there comes a time when we have to pull off the proverbial side of the road, come to a complete stop, and check under the hood because something just is not right. Both action points are critical to diagnosing what is actually happening. Too often, we have a sense that things might not be great, but we just keep trucking on down the road, blowing off all warning signs flashing right before our very eyes, wishfully hoping it will all just work itself out.

One of my sons had this same experience as a high school senior. An engine warning light had come on. We didn't respond quickly enough to stop driving the car immediately to try to figure out what was actually happening under the hood. The result: a blown head gasket and the need for a new engine. Not only was his vehicle out of operation for a lengthy period, but it took a pretty good blow to the pocketbook as well!

In life, this is a matter of not wanting to pull over and slow down. We often fear what we will find under our hood. We fear we might find that our life is a real mess, like a blown head gasket, which we can promise you will keep you stuck on the side of the road until you have given your engine the proper attention.

So when we lift the hood, what are we looking for? We are looking to examine whether the issue causing the problem does not lie without but within. Drew Brees, after a time of reflection and examination, gives us a great snapshot of what this looks like as he humbly acknowledged what he could have done differently to be part of the solution to the racial tensions that still exists in our country today.

As we reflect on what he said and how he quickly arrived at such a posture of humility and brokenness amidst such a public outcry, we have an example of how quickly broken relationships could begin to heal and recover from intense strife and division if we all had such a similar response of humility and repentance as well as a commitment to speak less and listen more to each other.

Fasting from Self and Feasting on Christ

So how do we arrive at this point? C. S. Lewis offers us this thought in *Mere Christianity*, "True humility is not thinking less of yourself; it is thinking of yourself less."[16] A heart poised toward others is constantly about the welfare of others, while a heart poised toward self is sure to cultivate suffocating pride. But it is not just diverting our focus from self, but deliberately and intentionally turning our gaze toward Christ. It is not until we can see God for who He is, as we see the depths of Christ's humility of service in going to the cross, as Philippians 2:6–8 depicts, that we then find our proper position and posture before God and others.

As we sit with the shadow of the cross covering us, we learn that nothing is beneath us in terms of service, and we can bask in His goodness and delight in following Him. This is true gospel humility, that Christ died for my sins and we are deeply dependent upon Him. In fact, it is what separates Christianity from all other religions to have as its central event the humiliation and the humility of its God.

The Standard for Humility

We can't miss this point! Just because we have heard this all our lives does not mean we can quickly brush over the magnitude of what Jesus did! Unfortunately, two thousand years of religious art and architecture have domesticated the image of the cross, stripping it of its historical shock and awe. Crucifixion was the ancient world's ultimate form of punishment.

There were three official methods of capital punishment: crucifixion, decapitation, and being burned alive, but crucifixion was regarded as the most brutal. In an honor-shame culture, early Christians took Jesus's crucifixion not as His humiliation but as proof that greatness can express itself in humility, the noble choice to lower yourself for the sake of others.[17] These first Christians could say or sing both "God" and the "cross" in the same breath! The idea that any great individual, particularly the Almighty, could be associated with the shameful Roman crucifixion is mind-blowing! This is a humility revolution!

Dickson in *Humilitas* said,

> Honor and shame are turned on its heads. The highly regarded Jesus lowered himself to a shameful cross, and yet, in so doing became the object of scorn but one of praise and emulation ... honor has been redefined, greatness recast. The shameful place is now a place of honor, the low point is the high point.[18]

And what then is the posture in which we see our Jesus? We find him bending low on his knees, washing the feet of his disciples.

Richard Simmons in *The True Measure of a Man* says,

> The biblical understanding is that the humble are the strongest. They do not make decisions by sticking their fingers in the air to see what other people think. They enjoy fortitude, an inner strength that comes

only through God's grace. They know who they are. Their lives are not consumed by trying to please and impress others.[19]

Without humility, pride will run wild throughout our lives.[20] We must decrease so Christ may increase in our lives (John 3:30).

The humility often thought of as weakness can now be redefined as strength. In the gospel of John, we read that John the Baptist was often mistaken as the Christ. Yet despite the fame he was attaining, he always redirected the glory to Jesus, saying that there is one who comes after him whose sandals he is unworthy to untie (John 2:26, 30). This is a man whom Jesus referred to as the greatest man born of a woman (Matthew 11:11).

In the same way that John redirects glory to Jesus, we see Jesus, the Son of God, redirect glory to the Father. In John 5, Jesus speaks twice about his dependency upon the Father and how He can do nothing on His own accord. If the only perfect Man to ever live and the greatest man born of a woman embodied this type of humility, it proves that true genuine strength is in fact found in humility.

Strength in Weakness

Humility then means boasting in our weakness. Simmons calls this "life's greatest paradox." When in culture are we ever told to delight in our weakness or expose our struggles? Culture tells men that they cannot be weak, yet "the Bible encourages an understanding of masculinity and Christlikeness that leads to both being vulnerable and delighting in weakness."[21] The apostle Paul did not find his weaknesses to be shameful, but rather to be embraced as it revealed the work of Christ in his life.[22] In fact, our humility should grow with the passing years, just like other qualities and attributes.

Notice Paul's development in his sense of self from his early to latter years. Early in his ministry, he said, "I am the least of the apostles, and do not even deserve to be called an apostle" (I

Corinthians 15:9 NIV). Later he offered, "I am less than the least of all God's people" (Ephesians 3:8 NIV). Then toward the end of his life, he spoke of God's sweet mercy to him as he said, "Christ Jesus came into the world to save sinners—of whom I am the worst" (1 Timothy 1:15 NIV).

Real men find themselves boasting in their weakness as it produces a humble and contrite heart that is dependent upon the Lord, thus creating a free spirit no longer living under bondage of the law but the freeing truth of the gospel!

In the words of John Piper, the beauty of "gospel humility is it frees you from the need to posture and pose and calculate what others think, so that you are free to laugh at what is really funny with the biggest belly laugh. Proud people don't really let themselves go in laughter. They don't get red in the face and fall off their chairs and twist their faces into contortions of real free laughter. Proud people need to keep their dignity. The humble are free to howl with laughter."[23]

True humility not only allows you the opportunity to let loose and laugh, but it also permits you to admit your shortcomings, even disastrous ones. A radical example of this is in the book *Extreme Ownership* by Navy Seals Jocko Willink and Leif Babin. In the first chapter, Jocko recalls their first engagement in Ramada, Iraq, when the fog of war had settled in as the smoke from grenades, clouds of dust from tanks and Humvees, and powdered concrete from walls pulverized by gunfire completely permeated the air. For pages, he describes the intensity of the gunfight as sides tore into each other behind concrete walls and barriers. But suddenly it became clear that the unthinkable, the mortal sin of a Seal Team or any military group, was unfolding right before their very eyes! They were engaged in a blue on blue! They were fighting friendly forces and didn't even know it! As quickly as fighting could be ceased, it was discovered that one friendly Iraqi soldier was dead and one of their own was wounded.

Immediately all were rushed back to base, and an investigative team with the commanding officer (CO) and the command master chief (CMC), who wanted answers, were sent to their base camp for an explanation. As they interviewed one man after another, they finally came to Jocko, the SEAL task unit commander of Task Unit Bruiser. What he said was going to determine not only the outcome of the investigation but the trajectory of his tenure and legacy in the military.

When given the opportunity, he said,

> You know whose fault this is? You know who gets all the blame for this? There is only one person to blame for this: me. I am the commander. I am responsible for the entire operation. As the senior man, I am responsible for every action that takes place on the battlefield. There is no one to blame but me. And I will tell you this right now: I will make sure that nothing like this ever happens to us again.[24]

Helping Others Along the Road

Once we are able to acknowledge that the greatest problem is not out there but rather is an internal issue to be revealed, repented of, and reconciled before God and often others, we are then ready to offer ourselves and our lives as the means of grace to help others in need.

In fact, C. S. Lewis in *Mere Christianity* notes that if we were to meet a truly humble person, we would never come away from meeting them thinking they were humble. They would not be telling us that they were a nobody (because a person who keeps saying they are a nobody is actually a self-obsessed person). Instead, if you met a true gospel-humble person, they would seem totally interested in you! Such a person is not thinking of how every experience, situation, and conversation connects to them. It is called the art of self-forgetfulness![25]

Paul David Tripp says that "Sin has left this world in a sorry condition. You see it everywhere you look" and Jesus "has asked you to move in with him to be one of his tools of restoration" and fight against the sin that is ravaging God's world.[26] It is only the gospel that can produce a humility that even gives us the notion that this is a good idea to "count others more significant than yourselves" (Philippians 2:3 ESV). To acknowledge and address our broken-down engine allows us to humbly help others also in need.

However, entering brokenness is no easy task. It is exhausting, intimidating, and unnerving, and it requires grace, patience, and a dependency upon the Lord. Even Jesus experienced the effects of entering brokenness. After long periods of teaching, healing, and pursuing relationships, Luke 5:16 notes that "Jesus often withdrew to lonely places and prayed" (NIV). But that never stopped him from pursuing restoration. Jesus physically entered into this world with the purpose of entering brokenness to bring about restoration. We see this through His teaching when He healed people with diseases and demons and when He ate with sinners like Zacchaeus.

Jesus is a perfect role model for how we ought to engage the sin in our world. Tripp refers to this world as a broken-down house.[27] It was once a beautifully constructed masterpiece, but through humanity's rebellion, it has been utterly destroyed, and as image-bearers and sons of God, we are called to participate in this restoration of all things.[28]

But the restoration of all things is much easier said than done. John Eldredge says, "The true essence of strength is passed to us from God through our union with him," and we are to use this strength for what God has called us to do.[29] Larry Crabb says that men were designed by God to move into the regions of this world that are dark and unpredictable.[30] True strength is found when we move into the unknown areas of life, regions that frighten us nonetheless and seek to restore it.

This is our calling because this is where we see Jesus. We find Him weeping over brokenness. One of the most powerful verses in scripture is John 11:35, "Jesus wept" (NIV). This is particularly profound for two reasons:

1. It shows that "Jesus is one with us in our need; he feels our pain; he lives our experience from the inside; [and] his tears

at that moment authentically expressed the emotion of his heart."[31]

2. We see how brokenness moves our Savior to tears as He mourns over sin.

A man who understood his place before God and in this world was Samuel Brengle, a commissioner of the Salvation Army and a leading author and teacher who lived in the late 1800s and early 1900s. When referred to as the great Doctor Brengle, he said,

> If I appear great in their eyes, the Lord is most graciously helping me to see how absolutely nothing I am without him, and helping me to keep little in my own eyes. He does use me. But I am so concerned that he does use me and that it is not of me the work is done. The axe cannot boast of the trees it has cut down. It could do nothing but for the woodsman. He made it, he sharpened it, and he used it. The moment he throws it aside, it becomes only old iron. O that I may never lose sight of this.[32]

"Martin Luther used a phrase in the 1520s that he said holds the whole church up, a phrase on which the church rises or falls. If someone gets this phrase, they get the gospel. If they lose it, they lose everything. That phrase was *simul iustus et peccator*: simultaneously righteous and a sinner. We remain sinners—humbled before God— but we are also declared righteous by God, given a confidence to come before his throne boldly."[33]

From this posture of humility and an understanding that we are in desperate need of internal evaluation and restoration, we must acknowledge that we are nothing apart from the work of Christ. Then we can, with enthusiasm and optimism, humbly venture forward toward this challenge of finding the masculine courage to stand to and act on our convictions.

Ten Statements for Reflection and Evaluation of One's Personal Humility

As you review and reflect on these statements, to the right, evaluate yourself using a one-to-five scale with (1) being poor and must improve and (5) being "by God's grace doing very well.

1. I actively listen and choose to speak less. _____
2. I often ask insightful questions of others. _____
3. I regularly exhibit a teachable spirit. _____
4. I readily admit and confess when wrong. _____
5. I accept insults and injuries with grace. _____
6. I do not seek to be admired and loved. _____
7. I ask others of blind spots in my life. _____
8. I deflect credit and praise to God and others. _____
9. I do not compare myself to others. _____
10. I give permission for others to disagree with me. _____

If you are honest with yourself, you will have concluded, like we did, that we are not nearly as humble as we ought to be. This can be overwhelming if convicted of the need for growth. Start by identifying the top (two to three) areas of most needed and desired growth in humility. Specifically commit to spend time daily asking the Lord for growth and grace in these areas. And ask someone close to you to offer encouragement and accountability to assist you in these areas of desired growth in humility. This person needs to be able to speak directly and honestly, knowing their words will be well-received and heeded.

This exercise will be important as many more challenges will be put in front of you over the following thirteen chapters. A humble response acknowledging areas of needed growth will serve you well as you read and wrestle with the content shared.

My oldest son, Joshua Brower, and I wrote Chapter One together. Part of this chapter is the work of Josh's Senior Integration Project (SIP) at Covenant College entitled *Becoming Men: A Biblical Guide for Redefining Masculinity.*

Josh Brower is a graduate of Covenant College with a degree in Biblical and Theological Studies / Youth Ministry. He is a former All-American soccer player and currently serves as the codirector of High School Ministry at Lookout Mountain Presbyterian Church on Lookout Mountain, Tennessee.

CHAPTER TWO

THE COURAGE CHALLENGE

Show yourself a man, and keep the charge of the Lord your God ...
—1 KINGS 2:2–3 (ESV)

The righteous are as bold as lions.
—PROVERBS 28:1 (ESV)

Courage is not simply one of the virtues, but the form of every virtue at the testing point, which means at the point of highest reality.[34]
—C. S. LEWIS

William Wallace (*Braveheart*), Jason Bourne, Aragorn (*Lord of the Rings*), members from Seal Team Six, and King David's Mighty Men could all provide great examples of performing incredible feats requiring masculine courage. However, to provide such examples from men as these could quickly discourage us from ever being able to measure up to such courageous men, whether real or fictional. So let me encourage your masculine heart to act with courage by offering an example from the life of a seventh-grade boy.

Courage from My Son

One morning on my way to work as a high school principal, my seventh-grade son turned to me and said, "Dad, I want to pray for the high school students."

I said, "Well, Jakob, that is great. Go ahead and do it as we drive to school."

He replied, "No, I mean at school."

"You mean you want to pray at ... like a chapel?" I asked.

"No, Dad, after the school chaplain gives the weekly devotion over the intercom, I want to come on and pray for the high school students."

Thinking that was really going to take guts as a young seventh grader, I asked if he really were sure he wanted to do that as his conviction and courage exceeded mine that morning as he emphatically said, "Absolutely, Dad."

After he asked the senior chaplain for permission, he took the intercom in hand and said to close to six hundred high school students, "Good morning, high school students. This is Jakob Brower, and I want to pray for you this morning. Please bow your heads and pray with me."

In this simple and yet courageous act, my seventh-grade son just answered the big life question as to whether he was becoming a man living out his God-designed maleness with courage or suppressing his unique design given by God. I know this sounds like I put my son in a box with these two distinct categories, but here's the distinction. A coward is a man who knows the right thing to do but allows fear to keep him from doing it. The courageous man knows the right thing to do and is equally fearful yet does it anyway. Acting in the face of fear is courage. Choosing not to act in the face of fear is the mark of a coward.

Notice that fear is present in both choices. It is why the show *Fear Factor* that aired years ago was something that caught so many people's attention because every challenge gripped contestants and onlookers alike with great fear. The question was whether they could overcome that fear.

The Ultimate Courage Example

It is important to point out that every action we take is not necessarily courageous. Some actions that appear courageous are purely reckless. Here is the difference. Courageous action is taken as a matter of principle and heart-level conviction. It is usually predictable and predetermined because it comes from a place of one's personally held belief system.

The greatest example ever was Jesus going to the cross. In the garden of Gethsemane, the Bible notes that He experienced what we know today as a rare condition called *hematidrosis*, which is brought on by the most extreme levels of fear and anxiety as he "sweat great drops of blood" at the thought of His flesh being ripped from his bones during His scourging, the nails being driven through His hands, and the spear being rammed through His side!

The anticipation and level of anxiety were so mind-blowing that He even asked His Father if He would relent and not make Him go through with the never-before task of dying on a cross and taking on the sins of the world. It was not just the anticipation of the pain but the searing loss of being separated from His Father—to being forsaken—to having His Father turn His back on him.

Being fully man as well, we get that, right? There were no hands raised or waiting lines for that job! And yet, as we know, Jesus walked right into the biggest mess, the world's greatest challenge, and He conquered death and the grave, the greatest victory known to the natural and supernatural world!

What do we learn from Jesus in this? It is not that he had eliminated fear, for if fear did not exist, there would be no need for courage! What we see is a deliberate and intentional choice to act. It was a surrender and dying to one's self for the benefit of others. Wait! Come on! There's got to be some special formula to being courageous! You are right. Here it is.

Courage Words from a King

Here is the reality! The much sought-after answer to true masculine courage has been right before us for centuries. However, if we have been looking to someone or something to define it for us other than God and His Word, we have been searching in all the wrong places. We see this come into full view when King David, a fighter, a man of war, a man after God's own heart, a warrior king looking to pass his kingship on to his son.

Before he dies, he calls Solomon to his side and deliberately tells him, "Be strong, and show yourself a man, and keep the charge of the Lord your God, walking in His ways and keeping His statutes, His commands, His rules, and His testimonies … that you may prosper in all that you do and wherever you turn" (1 Kings 2:2–3 ESV).

Six times King David directs his son Solomon toward God. David did not stop after "be strong and show yourself a man" because that would have left us wondering what that exactly might look like. Instead he offers clear, definitive action points for his son to follow. Keep or hold on to God's charge, ways, statutes, commands, rules, and testimonies, and then walk in those ways and not others.

In other words, act on the knowledge and the wisdom given to you from God. There it is! In order to act courageously, it will require movement out of you. You must move forward, make an advance, and step up. To act and move courageously is to believe in the depths of your being, with great conviction that something must happen even though fear is telling you to remain in the shadows a bit longer.

Masculinity Defined

So is courage something only for men? Absolutely not. However, in 1 Corinthians 16:13, we read of a definite distinction of our masculine uniqueness and design where Paul says, "Be watchful, stand firm in the faith, act like men, be strong" (ESV). This challenge to show and act like a man stands in contrast to acting like a boy or a woman. While gender is God-bestowed at birth, one cannot become more of that specific gender. A male is a male; a female is a female. We know this from God's creation in the garden despite our culture now saying there are over sixty different genders. So while a man is a man, he can certainly further develop the masculine nature of his gender. To become more masculine requires sustained hard work, discipline, and a very intentional effort that extends beyond just physical strength to also include strength of character, which would include integrity, honesty, loyalty, commitment and dedication, humility, and responsibility. Passivity, reluctancy, and laziness can play no part in the development and enhancement of one's masculinity. A masculine man will have to put his back, mind, and heart into what he is doing and engage in the good struggle of overcoming obstacles or challenges that lie before him. As he does so, traits such as diligence, perseverance, determination, and particularly courage embraced and practiced will begin to shape and define the masculine nature and course of a man's life. C. S. Lewis said, "Courage is not simply one of the virtues, but the form of every virtue at the testing point."[35]

It makes no difference in a man's masculine physical strength if he does not have the courage to act upon that strength. A man cannot lead, love, provide, and defend to his full potential without the application of exemplary courage. No culture can endure where lazy men are celebrated, cowardly men are esteemed, insecure men are elevated, or non-principled men are leading for very long. Proverbs 28:1 says, "The righteous are as bold as lions!" (ESV). So the heart of a lion is needed to stand firm on your convictions and to act! Why are the godly bold as lions? The answer is because the godly know they are backed by truths of Scripture written by men inspired by the Great Warrior King, God Himself. Truth gives spines and backbones to spineless, fear-filled men because they know they have the backing and boldness of the King. And if the King is backing us, then we should reflect His image as the Great Lion of Judah!

The Greek and Masculinity Defined

To take an even deeper dive into examining this intersection of courage and masculinity, let's look at the ancient Greeks. For the Greeks, the word *andreia* meant courage, derived from the root word *andros*, which means man. Courage and *andreia* can also be translated as manliness or the essence of masculinity itself.

To the Greeks, the primary tool of their masculine trade was in the wielding of a tested sword. The sword in the hand of the blacksmith was forged, refined, and proven before it became a sword. However, the sword was much more than just a tool; it was also a symbol of one's masculine journey of being forged through hardship, yet standing tall in the face of adversaries, imposters, counterfeits, and conflict.[36] With the gender confusion seen through modern society's redefining of masculinity, the ancient Greeks help us to reorient our thinking about masculinity and the expectation to exercise courage. However, we don't have to merely look to the ancient Greeks for clarity on this matter.

Courageous Women

While I have given several examples of what masculine courage is, it might be good to see what happens when men are expected to act like men and they abdicate their responsibilities. When this happens, women have to step in and fill the vacuum of needed courageous action where it is expected of men.

We see this in Judges 4 when Israel had a female judge named Deborah. At the time, the Canaanites had oppressed Israel for twenty years. Deborah called Barak to her and essentially asked him if he was ready to go and defeat General Sisera (Judges 4:6–7). That she had to ask him this question shows that he already was reluctant, but Barak had a great opportunity to step up and do the required noble and courageous task. Instead Barak replied, "If you go with me, I will go, but if you don't go with me, I will not go" (vs. 8 NIV).

To this she replied, "I will surely go with you. Nevertheless, the road on which you are going will not lead to your glory, for the Lord will sell Sisera into the hand of a woman" (vs. 9 ESV).

Whoa, come on, Barak! In simple terms, she tells him, "Since you have acted like a coward and have not done the task God gave you to do, by default, a woman is going to have to step up and do your dirty work for you!" In even plainer terms, Deborah had to take Barak's man card and lead him by the hand.

In the end, Jaal, a woman, killed Sisera as she took a tent peg and "drove the peg into his temple until it went down into the ground while he was lying fast asleep from his weariness. So he died" (vs. 21 ESV).

While Jaal is certainly not a woman to mess with and should be talked about more than she is, I can't help but think that Barak had to be embarrassed that Jaal had done the job he was supposed to have done. Come on, Barak! Man up!

Yet if I am honest, in a moment of self-reflection, I have to admit that, like Barak, there are times I too don't do the job that God has entrusted to me and that my wife needs me to do. We can be sitting at the dinner table eating our meal and the boys can begin arguing with each other, or I can be working on my computer in the living room and the boys start wrestling with each other where punches start getting thrown and bodies are flying. Then I will get that look from my wife as if to say, "Um, are you not seeing any of this? Hello, like now would be a great time for you to intervene before food is thrown, someone starts bleeding, or bones are broken."

Not an Excuse ... But Not Helpful

Just as there is a difference in the design, roles, and expectations between men and women, there is a distinction between the makeup of true men and boys. Sure they are similar biologically, but beyond that, there is little else the same. However, as we look at many of the movies and television shows that Hollywood is producing today, what we see is men acting more like immature boys instead of men acting like mature men! In fact, what we see is a pathetic version of men that are not to be taken seriously. Back in 2011, Nicole Johnson in "The Depressing Depiction of Men in the Media" writes,

> Here's what I find tremendously disconcerting: Hollywood has started writing and producing content which depicts men as ridiculous and as people who should not be taken seriously. The characterizations of men in the media over the past two decades portray men as weak and incompetent. Interestingly enough, it's men who are behind the scenes doing this, not women. Hollywood is a notorious "boy's club." Clearly the men creating movies such as *Knocked Up, Old School, The 40 Year Old Virgin, Pineapple Express, Super Bad, The Hangover, Forgetting Sarah Marshall,* and *I Love You, Man* are simply seeing dollar signs. What man would walk away from these movies saying, *"I want to be like him?"* Conversely, what woman would walk away saying, *"I want to marry him?"* I understand it's designed to be entertaining, but if I were a man, I'd be horrified.[37]

The perceptive dumbing down of the American male made to appear more inept and less competent or capable has an increasingly higher appeal to the American public with the result that our young men fall prey to supporting and mimicking this type of absurd behavior.

Act Like a Man

This is the messaging that our young men and you are bombarded with every day. This is why God's Word, not the media, must inform us and be our guide of who we are and who we are called to be. Paul provides clarity and a marked distinction between boys and men that amplify his statement to "act like men." In 1 Corinthians 13:11, he states, "When I was a child, I spoke like a child, I thought like a child, I reasoned like a child. When I became a man, I gave up childish ways" (ESV).

In this one brief yet comprehensive verse, Paul reinforces his statement to "act like men" that would entail a clear breaking away from and embracing a difference as established by God in how one thinks, speaks, reasons, and then acts.

Paul provides further direction for us with regards to how a man is to act for and toward his wife and children as a man is to offer strength as a leader to his wife (Ephesians 5:23) and a provider for his family (1 Timothy 5:8) even in the face of adversity and great struggle. In fact, in Hebrews 12:12–13a we see the writer throwing down a challenge almost as if to say, "Don't have a pity party for yourself. Man up and just do it." We need your strength and courage as he writes, "Therefore lift your drooping hands and strengthen your weak knees, and make straight paths for our feet …" (ESV).

While there are other similar passages in Scripture to support this, it is clear that to man up and to courageously act like a man or to show yourself to be a man means to be one who is clearly both grounded, growing, and living out his faith through the transforming process of intentionally following after God and not conforming to the patterns of this world (Romans 12:2). Psalm 37:23 reiterates this thinking by declaring, "The steps of a man are established by the Lord, when he delights in his way" (ESV).

Men firmly grounded and consistently growing in God's Word will radically change not just marriages, family units, and local communities but the entire trajectory of a nation. We know this from Psalm 33:12 where the psalmist declares to his son, "Blessed is the nation whose God is the Lord!" (ESV). This happened in America over two hundred years ago, and it needs to happen once again. This is why it is necessary for men today to "man up and step up" by being immersed in God's Word and letting it be their constant guide as they take courageous action.

If I Die, I Die

Our God-designed maleness to courageously act must press us forward where fear and conviction converge. It is one thing to know what to do; it is an entirely other matter to actually act on it. Let me illustrate, but not by using an example of a giant-slayer but of a beautiful young girl named Esther from the Bible.

After Esther won a national beauty pageant and became the Queen of Persia to King Artaxerxes, one day her Uncle Mordecai refused to bow to Haman, who at that time was second-in-command to the king. In Haman's fury at Mordecai, he was able to convince the king to issue an edict to eradicate all the Jews in one day. This would be a modern-day version of the movie *The Purge*! When Mordacai heard this, he ran to Ester and told her that she must go and talk to the king, who was oblivious that his new queen was also a Jew. Yet she knew that to go before the king without him summoning her could mean immediate death.

However, Mordacai said, "If you keep silent, help will come from somewhere else, but you too will die … And who knows whether you have not come to the kingdom for such a time as this?"

But hear this! In Esther 4:16, Esther concluded, "I will go to the king, though it is against the law, and if I perish, I perish!" (ESV). This truly is courage that sprang up from a deep heart conviction that overrides potential consequences.

The Cost of Silence

So the natural question is: what is the cost for you to keep silent? You are probably aware that there is a cost if you speak up as a Christian. That is very true. We know this is what we should expect! In Mark 13:13 Jesus gives us a pep talk on this issue when He says, "All men will hate you because of me, but he who stands firm to the end will be saved" (ESV).

In Luke 6:22, Jesus says, "Blessed are you when men hate you, when they exclude you, and insult you, and reject you ... because of the Son of Man" (NIV). However, remember who you are, what you have been given, and what you have been called to do as a man! Maybe you have been, like Esther, providentially placed in your circumstance and situation for this very moment in which you find yourself. Perhaps you stand at a crossroads and there is a decision to make. Possibly your very life has been culminating to this very specific moment in time.

Don't miss it to just stand on the sidelines! Might you have the same resolve as this young Jewish girl to be able to say with great conviction, "If I die, I die," but it is always the right time to do the right thing even if everyone is against it!

Let's Roll

On that unforgettable day, September 11, 2001, United Flight 93 was hijacked. Passenger Todd Beamer on a cell phone call told GTE air phone supervisor that the hijackers had killed the pilots and that several passengers were planning to jump on the hijackers and fly the plane into the ground before they could follow through on their plan. Beamer recited the Lord's Prayer and Psalm 23 with the operator and then requested, "If I don't make it, please call my family and let them know how much I love them."

After this, Beamer said to others joining in the plan, "Are you ready? Okay. Let's roll." These were Beamer's last known words as he and others courageously surrendered their lives in an attempt to stop the terrorist hijackers.

Astonishing Courage

So why is this book *Stand To: Finding Masculine Courage in a Stand Down World*? I write this for you to serve as a challenge to engage and act with courage and boldness in your everyday lives, situations, and circumstances in which God has placed you. The opportunities are all around you. You don't have to have a doctorate degree, have studied for years in the ministry, or even hold an office in your church.

Listen to the words from Acts 4:13 after two young men, Peter and John, finished talking to those who accused them of causing trouble as they preached about Jesus. "When they saw the courage of Peter and John and realized that they were unschooled, ordinary men, they were astonished and they took note that these men had been with Jesus!" (NIV).

There it is! No excuses for us, ordinary, unschooled but courageous men who had spent some time with Jesus. We have no idea what would be in store for our communities and our country if ordinary guys like you and me were to courageously stand as Peter, John, and others have done through history! Each of us should be warned that we all have a bit of Barak in us where our true strength goes underground, sabotaging a world of potential, and, in the end, fails to be put to good use. For that reason, I intentionally used a couple examples of women who acted courageously. Good, strong women will step in when passive, weak, and reluctant men won't. We each have a backbone and should use it, courageously offering strength for the betterment of others to the glory of God! To turn the next page is to accept this masculine challenge to act like men!

So as you consider turning the page and embarking on this

journey toward courage, allow me to use the words of wise Bilbo Baggins, repeated by Frodo to his best friend Sam, "It's a dangerous business, Frodo, going out your door. You step onto the road, and if you don't keep your feet, there's no knowing where you might be swept off to."

While uncertainty is around the corner, the opportunities to fully embrace your masculine, courageous design ought to draw you in and compel you to step forward with great certainty and resolve. It's your move. What will you do? Step down and lose ground or stand to and push through? Choose wisely, my friend!

CHAPTER THREE

MY LIFE CREED

[Join with me] in suffering as a good soldier of Christ Jesus.
—2 TIMOTHY 2:3–4 (ESV)

God has fixed the time of my death. I do not concern myself about that, but to be always ready, no matter when it may overtake me ... That is the way all men should live, and then all would be equally brave."[38]
—STONEWALL JACKSON

I Believe!

The "I believe ... I believe that ... I believe that we ... I believe that we will win, I believe that we will win ..." cadence reverberated from one side of the stadium to the other. From the intense chanting and enthusiastic synchronized jumping to the dramatic faces on overzealous fans, I could not believe the fervor and passion I was witnessing. Fans vowed their allegiance and support for their national soccer team playing against a rival country in a manner that appeared to be a life-or-death matter!

This simple "I believe" chant has quickly become the most trending chant in sports today. It was only back in 1998 that Jay Rodriguez was tasked to come up with a cheer for his fifty-member platoon at a Naval Academy prep school. It did not take long before

ESPN created multiple "I believe that we will win" commercials that served as the battle cry for the US National Soccer Team preparing for the 2014 World Cup.[39]

While this chant certainly is contagious and can create a frenzied environment for the athletic enthusiast, it is shouted with a great deal of hype and wishful thinking and ultimately can only offer hope as its highest aim.

If I were to ask you what you believe in, I suspect you would give me a list of beliefs that draw upon areas of deep passion, places of great enthusiasm, personal conviction, and engagement and are the basis for debate, decisions you make, and hopefully definitive action on your part. Over the years, groups of people have drawn up what are referred to as creeds that explicitly detail their most deeply held convictions and beliefs. The Latin word for creed is *credo*, which simply means "I believe."

Military Creedal Living

Each branch of our military has developed a creed. These creeds are not just simply to be memorized, recited, and embraced as merely nice ideals. Instead creeds are meant to be embedded and intertwined into the very fibers of one's personhood so that when confronted with a reality that is contrary to the deeply held creedal belief, there will be no doubting, lingering, or questioning, but instead instinctive and ensuing deliberate action. For our armed forces, this means to defend our country and fight the enemy at the expense of one's very life.

I will long remember in 2012 when one of my former high school students, who upon graduation from college, was married and deployed to Afghanistan all within one month. In his first week, while on a patrol, his unit came under heavy fire from the Taliban forces, and as Andrew Smith jumped over a wall, he landed on a pressure plate that detonated an IED. As as result, Andrew lost both of his legs from the knee down. However, it was not just his legs he lost, but shrapnel from the explosion ripped through him and slashed apart his abdomen. Infection almost killed him. Doctors performed fifteen surgeries on his intestines.

Months after his release from Walter Reed Medical Center in Maryland, with his new prosthetic legs and accompanied by his wife, Andrew came back home and spoke to our school's student body. In a question-and-answer session, I recall a student asking him if he could, would he go back to Afghanistan to fight the Taliban again. I remember thinking at that very moment, *What an insensitive and maybe inappropriate question after all Andrew has been through.*

However, without hesitating or wavering in the slightest, Andrew, with resolve in his voice, quickly said, "I absolutely would go back!"

Now drawn in, the student pressed further and asked him why, knowing full well of the great cost possibly awaiting him.

Again, Andrew responded with such clarity, affirmation, and resolve by confidently saying, "I absolutely would go back to keep the fight there and to stop it from coming to America, the country I love!"

Andrew, my former student, became my hero that day!

Warrior Creeds

After reading the Army's creed, "The Soldier's Creed," I was even more moved. Andrew's response that day was not just something that he thought would be a good patriotic thing to say. Instead, when the Army had him learn these words, "I stand ready to deploy, engage, and destroy the enemies of the United States of America in close combat. I am a guardian of freedom and the American way of life. I am an American Soldier,"[40] at some point Andrew embraced them as his own. In fact, it was not fear that gripped Andrew as the Taliban's bullets whizzed overhead. Instead it was his sincere conviction in his mission as he moved toward the fight, the chaos, and the danger zone—not away from it.

Today, Andrew embodies the Wounded Warrior Creed that states,

Though I am wounded, I will always be a warrior,
I will never give up, nor quit in the face of adversity.
I will do my best in all that I do and achieve.
I will not allow my injuries to limit me, and most of all,
I will never forget my fallen comrades or leave
a fellow injured warrior behind.[41]

The aforementioned creeds and those that follow are all born out of conflict, pain, and great struggle. A wounded marine wrote the Wounded Warrior Creed in 2005 as he lay wracked by personal pain in a hospital, only to be consumed by indescribable agony, loss, and hopelessness. Steve R. Watt penned *The Soldier's Creed* as he reflected on his time in the "Special Forces and the S.W.A.T. alongside deadly and dangerous men with whom he shared fear, sweat, and blood. He emphasized that these were men committed to the cause of liberty, who believed that it was worth everything they had to give—even their lives."[42] Specifically the writing followed the loss of a good friend in the service who had left behind a young family.

William Tyler Page wrote the *American Creed* in 1917 during the middle of World War I. Though brief, it pulls in phrases from twelve key United States documents, like the Constitution, the Gettysburg Address, and the Declaration of Independence, to unify a nation that defines who we are and what we believe is so worth fighting for, even if that means to sacrifice our very lives!

As I read each of these creeds, I find them inspiring, motivating, and full of perspective and purpose for a life worth living. However, even more than these words, I am drawn to know more about the authors whose life stories were shaped and marked by the words lived and realized. Unfortunately we live in a world of wimpy, paralyzed, drifting, disengaged, desensitized, bored, directionless, indecisive, boyish adults. C. S. Lewis accurately expressed men without chests in *Abolition of Man* when he said, "We make men without chests and expect of them virtue and enterprise. We laugh at honour and are shocked to find traitors in our midst. We castrate and bid the geldings be fruitful."[43]

I find myself standing and applauding these men of creed, courage, and conviction who knew themselves and their purpose and found meaning in their existence. As you read the creeds, remember these are written by men who have engaged in the conflict, faced great odds, overcome and pressed through adversity, and suffered great loss. Drink deeply of words that were penned over tear-stained papers as the passion and conviction overflow from experiences forever etched into the hearts and minds of men!

One Warrior's Creed, Steven R. Watt
If today is to be THE DAY, so be it.
If you seek to do battle with me this day you will
receive the best that I am capable of giving.
It may not be enough, but it will be everything that I have to give
and it will be impressive for I have constantly
prepared myself for this day.
I have trained, drilled and rehearsed my actions so that
I might have the best chance of defeating you.
I have kept myself in peak physical condition,
schooled myself in the martial skills
and have become proficient in the application of combat tactics.
You may defeat me, but you will pay a severe price
and will be lucky to escape with your life.
You may kill me, but I am willing to die if necessary.
I do not fear Death, for I have been close enough to it on
enough occasions that it no longer concerns me.
But I do fear the loss of my Honor and would rather die
fighting than to have it said that I was without **Courage**.
So I WILL FIGHT YOU, no matter how insurmountable
it may seem, and to the death if need be, in order that it
may never be said of me that I was not a Warrior.[44]

The Soldier's Creed
I am an American Soldier.
I am a Warrior and a member of a team.

I serve the people of the United States and live the Army Values.
I will always place the mission first.
I will never accept defeat.
I will never quit.
I will never leave a fallen comrade.
I am disciplined, physically and mentally tough, trained
and proficient in my warrior tasks and drills. I always
maintain my arms, my equipment and myself.
I am an expert and I am a professional.
I stand ready to deploy, engage, and destroy the enemies
of the United States of America in close combat.
I am a guardian of freedom and the American way of life.
I am an American Soldier.

The American Creed, William Tyler Page

I believe in the United States of America as a government of
the people, by the people, for the people; whose just powers
are derived from the consent of the governed, a democracy
in a republic, a sovereign Nation of many sovereign States; a
perfect union, one and inseparable; established upon those
principles of freedom, equality, justice, and humanity for
which American patriots sacrificed their lives and fortunes.
I therefore believe it is my duty to my country to love it,
to support its Constitution, to obey its laws, to respect
its flag, and to defend it against all enemies.[45]

To read the creeds of the Air Force, Coast Guard, Marines, Ranger, and Navy, go to the appendix. Interwoven into almost all these creeds echo the following bold statements:

1. The creed we embrace will give missional clarity, focus, and definitive life purpose.
2. Life is a battle, and we are called to offer strength and exercise masculine courage.
3. Our life is to be lived as a sacrifice for others.
4. Freedom is costly, conflict is expected, and death is possible.

5. We are in it to win it! Surrender is not an option! We must *stand to* and engage!

History offers us examples of such valiant men of courage, conviction, and commitment. Their faith and trust in the Almighty Sovereign Creator and King, who had providentially ordained all the events of their lives, allowed them to live each day to the fullest as soldiers of Christ.

Recall the words of Stonewall Jackson who stated that he felt "as safe in battle as in bed." Jackson was so bold in battle and cited the following as his rationale for how he went about his work as an officer in the Civil War, "God has fixed the time of my death. I do not concern myself about that, but to be always ready, no matter when it may overtake me ... That is the way all men should live, and then all would be equally brave."[46]

In a similar manner, George Washington was engaged in multiple battles from which, on many occasions, he never should have emerged alive. After having two horses shot out from under him, his jacket riddled by four bullet holes, and one battle where he was the only officer not wounded, he summed up his battlefield experience to his brother in this way, "I now exist and appear in the land of the living by the miraculous care of Providence, that protected me beyond all human expectation." [47]

In commenting on creeds, the late theologian R. C. Sproul stated,

> Throughout church history it has been necessary for the church to adopt and embrace creedal statements to clarify the Christian faith and to distinguish true content from error and false representations of the faith. Such creeds are distinguished from Scripture in that Scripture is *norma Normans* ("the rule that rules"), while the creeds are *norma normata* ("a rule that is ruled").[48]

The Rule That Rules

Creeds in the early church are not to be mistaken with modern-day company mission statements that hang in some nice picture frame on an office wall. The earliest Christian creed is found in the New Testament, which declared "Jesus is Lord." This might sound too simple, and while important, why would I draw this out? Context is everything. R. C. Spoul explains, "The loyalty oath required by Roman citizens to demonstrate their allegiance to the empire in general and to the emperor in particular was to say publicly, '*Kaisar Kurios*,' that is, 'Caesar is lord.'"[49]

Up to that point, Christians did everything in their power to follow civil law. However, to say "Caesar is lord" would be to force Christians to go against their good conscience, and this could not be done. Therefore to say instead "Jesus is Lord" was to evoke the wrath of Rome and often would result in their death. For early Christians then, creeds like the Apostles' Creed and the Nicene Creed were vital to give an outline of basic essential teachings that affirmed certain truths and separated themselves from heretical teachings. While such creeds are not exhaustive of everything they believe, everything written in these creeds they wholeheartedly believe and embrace. In fact, early creeds like the Apostles' Creeds served several purposes:

1. They were a confession of what they believed as truth is proclaimed and protected from false truths creeping in.
2. They served as an instrument to disciple others.
3. They were meant to bring about unity and bind a group of people together.

As my pastor, Pastor Harry Reeder, stated when speaking on the Apostles' Creed, "Who and what we worship will determine how we live, and how we live will determine who and what we worship." The words found in one's creed and the subsequent following actions of a man will reveal one's heart affections and ultimately their worship.

This is why in a world where the highest authority is often self, where good and evil and right and wrong are no longer opposites and where ethics and morality are subjective, there must be a return to Scripture, our God-designed masculinity, and the courage to pursue after them in the quest for our true manhood! Any other version of manhood is a house of cards built on one's own thoughts and ideas that will not stand the test of time nor the scrutiny and adversity that true men must encounter and endure.

A creed deriving its truth from God's word must serve as the *norma Normans*, or the highest authority, that gives way to a set of beliefs that govern and direct our actions and daily lives. Permit me to return to my summary of the creeds I included on earlier pages. You can't make the declarative statements and hold to vague, diluted, relativistic, morally weak, self-constructed values, principles, and beliefs.

1. The creed we embrace will give missional clarity, focus, and definitive life purpose.
2. Life is a battle, and we are called to offer strength and exercise masculine courage.
3. Our life is to be lived as a sacrifice for others.
4. Freedom is costly, conflict is expected, and death is possible.
5. We are in it to win it! Surrender is not an option! We must stand to and engage!

Stand To Be Strong

As Christians, we are instructed to "be strong in the Lord, and in his mighty power" (Ephesians 6:10 NIV). We don't need to run to our foxholes at the first sound of whizzing bullets. We do not need to give way to fear. Too often we read these first words "be strong" and they stop us dead in our tracks as we are gripped with fear to make our next move.

Look at the rest of the verse. It tells us how to be strong in the power of His might. Here is the great consolation: the outcome of the battle rests on God's performance, not on your skill or strength, and that makes all the difference!

As Christians, we are called to a life of active duty, not a life of ease. We are not called to be a summer soldier, but to live a rigorous life exposed to the elements of an enlisted soldier at war on the front lines as a battle-tested warrior, one who is willing to stand to and be ready for whatever comes his way. Are you starting to get a fuller picture of a man living well with masculine courage?

My hope is that after reading this chapter, something is welling up inside of your spirit that is causing you to lean in and throw your shoulders back and be ready to engage. If that describes you now, I am not surprised because that is how you have been designed. That is your true self fighting against your flesh and sin nature that wants to denounce your design. Don't listen! It is an imposter and a traitor that wants to prohibit you from being the man you are and the man you can become.

As you quicken your step and press forward, I must warn you that what lies before you is not for the cowards or weak of heart, but for the true courageous warriors whose strength and identity are founded and grounded in the person and work of Jesus Christ who knew great pain and anguish and yet fulfilled his life mission on the cross!

Courage Challenge

You have been given many excellent examples of creeds that have provided focus, purpose, and motivation to individuals and groups of people. Now it's your turn to write your own personal creed. Some may refer to it as a life mission statement, but for our purposes, let's refer to it as our personal creed.

By this point, you understand that the point is not to have this nice statement written on a piece of paper or in a beautiful frame hanging on a wall, but instead these deep personal convictions are meant to daily extract your masculine courage and to compel and propel you to be a man of action. A solid credal statement will provide you the clarity, structure, and sense of significance that your life is/ has counted or mattered.

To this end, it is vital to wrestle with the following questions and to be able to support your responses with Scripture. I can't emphasize enough that this personal creed statement must be birthed from God's Word as given to us and applied through our lives. You must answer these questions:

1. **Who Am I?** This specifically speaks to your identity. Our fingerprints are unique to us individually. They are a physical mark of our identity. What about your personal identity? What defines who you are? Imagine if the cross of Jesus Christ was the most dominant marking of who we are? The apostle Paul speaks of us as being "in Christ" over 160 times alone in his epistles. To have your identity in Christ means that you're placing your confidence for life and eternity in the Lord Jesus Christ. To be in Christ means you're learning to do all you do with and for Jesus in the kingdom of God. It means that you're being formed into the image of Jesus Christ and you want other people to see Jesus when they look at you. To understand this identity changes everything and allows you to begin to think and live purposefully as well as wrestle with questions, like the ones following.

2. **Why am I here?** This speaks to purpose.

   a. Who do I do it for? To know and believe in the depths of your being, who you are as an image-bearer of God, one found in Christ, a chosen adopted son of the Great King, one forgiven and redeemed by the blood of the Lamb, being sanctified day by day and conformed into the image of Jesus Christ, will provide clarity for who you ultimately work for. Acts 17:28 states, "In him we live and move and have our being" (ESV). Any other starting point will throw us off-kilter. Can you say that Jesus Christ is my Lord and Master, my highest authority, and that I will follow His command rules and submit to His will for my life? Every other boss, company, organizational chart, or personal creed that does not first see Christ as the lead Commander-in-Chief will begin with a faulty starting point. And if your starting point is off, your trajectory in a very short time will dramatically be off course, leaving you floundering at best.

b. How do I do what I do? To understand who you are and who you ultimately work for will then shape and directly impact what you do. Paul says, "So, whether you eat or drink, or whatever you do, do all to the glory of God" (1 Corinthians 10:31 ESV). You see, what you do does not so much matter as long as you can emphatically say and model that you are doing it clearly for the glory of God. In 1 Corinthians 10:31, Paul writes, "whatever you do, do it all for the glory of God" (NIV). *Whatever* is a comprehensive word with regards to our life calling. However, the constant caveat is that we do it for God's glory as we see Paul emphasize in 2 Corinthians 5:9, "So ... we make it our goal to please Him" (ESV). In Philippians 1:20, Paul drives this home further when he declares, "It is my eager expectations and hope that I will not be at all ashamed, but that with full courage now as always Christ will be honored (magnified) in my body, whether by life or by death" (ESV). Paul completely gets it! But notice how he emphasizes full courage. Half courage doesn't work. Your entire being must be committed, and you must be all in.

c. What value am I bringing? To add another layer after understanding who you are, who you ultimately work for, and how you should do what you do, you can begin to unpack what value you bring to the table. As an image-bearer of God, each of us possesses different gifts, talents, and abilities to be applied to the specific roles and responsibilities that have been extended to us. We are to steward each of these well for God's glory. As you work through these important questions, you should begin to catch more than just a glimpse, but a vibrant picture of what your life's purpose is! I would encourage you to write down the gifts and abilities God has entrusted to you. (When we live with joy and energy from those things we enjoy and do well, our lives not only have meaning but are lived with enthusiasm and vigor.) Read 1 Corinthians 12:12–31, 1 Peter 4:10, James 1:17, Luke 6:38, and Ephesians 4:4–16

3. Where am I going? This speaks to your life meaning. Here is where you may begin to write down specific goals or life outcomes you want to achieve in life while keeping in mind your identity, who you ultimately give account to, and the value you offer to others. It would be well worth your time to look up the following passages as you consider personal direction and life meaning: Psalm 37:4–6; Psalm 33:11; Proverbs 16:9; Philippians 3:14; Proverbs 3:5–6; Proverbs 16:3; Psalm 127:1; Proverbs 19:21; Proverbs 29:18; Luke 14:28; Romans 12:2; John 6:27; and Psalms 20:4.

Additional helpful steps to equip you to write your own personal creed would be to:

1. Consider the various **roles** in which God has ordained that we should walk (father, husband, career role, coach, etc.) and how you would want to be remembered in these roles. (This speaks to legacy and the eternal investments from your life) (2 Timothy 4:6–8; Psalm 145:4; Psalm 78:4; Deuteronomy 6:5–7). You might be thinking, *It is too early. I'm not even married!* or *It's too late. My children are nearly gone from the home!* You might be thinking, *I sure wish*

I had done this earlier, but now it is too late. If you are breathing, it is never too late! Start this today. It will change your life tomorrow.

2. As you consider what should be included in your life creed, it is important to also reflect on or examine the lives of others. What is it about their character, values, achievements, personality, or how they simply lived their lives that you would desire to emulate? Ask yourself, Why are these things of value to me? What from others' lives do I wish to include as part of my own personal creed? (Luke 6:40; Galatians 5:22; Hebrews 10:24–25; 1 Corinthians 11:1).

3. Finally, begin to craft your personal creed. Keep it simple, clear, and brief. It could be a solid paragraph or contain bullet points. What you express is more important than how you craft it. Focus on positive affirming statements you desire in life. Now write, "My Life Creed Is:

4. Likely the core of this creed you have just written will remain if you do it well and spend intentional time crafting it. However, it well may be organic as over time you reflect and refine this statement. Know that this is not an easy task. Things of great value do not come cheaply or quickly. However, if done well, you will never regret having gone through this process. It will direct or possibly redirect your life's trajectory. For most of us, we will slowly turn around and look down this long path we have traveled on in this journey of life. What will be of

lasting value and significance that will continue after you are gone? Think on this wherever you are on this journey. When men reflect on this question late in life, they are often filled with regret. Don't be one of those men! As you consider these future days of reflection, you can determine now what the review session will look like. Will you be able to say like Paul to Timothy, "I have fought the good fight, I have finished the race, I have kept the faith?" (2 Timothy 4:7 NIV).

CHAPTER FOUR

BATTLE-SCARRED ... AND STILL IN THE FIGHT

We must go through many hardships to enter the kingdom of God.
—ACTS 14:22 (NIV)

A war between the Saint and Satan (is) so bloody a one,
that the cruelest war which was ever fought by men, will
be found but sport and child's play to this ... The stage
whereon this war is fought, is every man's own soul.[50]
—WILLIAM GURNALL

A Dark Day

In *Lament for a Son*, Nicholas Wolterstorff took up the pen to attempt to describe his deep penetrating anguish of losing his twenty-five-year-old son to a climbing accident. He writes,

> Will my eyes adjust to this darkness? Will I find you
> in the dark—not in the streaks of light which remain,
> but in the darkness? Has anyone ever found you there?
> Did they love what they saw? Did they see love? And

43

are there songs for singing when the light has gone dim? Or in the dark, is it best to wait in silence?

Noon has darkened. As fast as they could say, "He's dead," the light dimmed. And where are you in the darkness? I learned to spy you in the light. Here in this darkness, I cannot find you. If I had never looked for you, or looked but never found, I would not feel this pain of your absence. Or is not your absence in which I dwell, but your elusive troubling presence?

It's the neverness that is so painful. Never again to be here with us—never to sit with us at the table ... All the rest of our lives we must live without him. Only our death can stop the pain of his death.[51]

Hard Providence

After spending a significant amount of time working through your personal convictions to develop your life creed, we need to talk about what the Puritans referred to as the hard providence of God. Puritan John Owen writes,

> Sorrows create a grave dilemma for the Christian, for he does not want to deny either the sovereignty or the goodness of God. If we desire to walk humbly with our God (Micah 6:8), then we must fall down before God and acknowledge that He has the sovereign right to do as He pleases. We must believe that He acts with wisdom, righteousness, goodness, love, and mercy in all that He does, even though it may be difficult to see that in confusing vicissitudes (change of circumstances), dizzying changes, and deep distress of life.[52]

We see King David in Psalm 39:9 writing, "I am mute; I do not open my mouth, for you who have done it" (ESV). Thomas Boston understood this when he said, "Whatever is crooked in life was made so by God and therefore must be received in submission to God. There is not anything whatsoever befalls us without his over-ruling hand."[53]

Ecclesiasticus 7:13 states, "Consider the work of God: who can make straight what He has made crooked?" (ESV) While I don't believe this is a call for us to be silent under great distress, for we most certainly can groan to a God who hears and comforts us, it should not be confused with grumbling.

In the *Works of John Knox*, the Elizabethan bishop, Thomas Cooper, spoke of the providence of God in this way, "That which we call fortune is nothing but the hand of God, working by causes and for causes that we know not. Chance or fortune are gods devised by man and made by our ignorance of the true, almighty and everlasting God."[54]

For each of us, we do not know exactly what the great battle is wherein we must engage. However, what is certain is that the battle is real and cannot be avoided and we must be engaged.

Puritan William Gurnall said it well when he wrote,

> A war between the Saint and Satan (is) so bloody a one, that the cruelest war which was ever fought by men, will be found but sport and child's play to this … The stage whereon this war is fought, is every man's own soul. There is no neutral in this war, the whole world is engaged in the quarrel, either for God against Satan, or for Satan against God.[55]

Life's Big Moments

We know that war is brutal, casualties are the by-product, lives are forever altered, and searing pain brands memories that recalibrate one's thinking and processing and form a new view on a now-shattered life. Time offers partial and gradual healing, but scars remain as wounds become windows we view and doorways we wincingly step through as we search for our new normal that is everything but normal. Libraries of books are written to depict the atrocities of war. The imagery, intensity, volume of agony, despair, and loss compressed into short segments of time is indescribable and often unbearable. Yet survivors must bear the pressing weight of present realities.

Like with Walterstorff, life's big moments can smash into us like a tidal wave that seems to plunge us beneath the surf's roll and then pin us to the ocean's floor, only to release us to the surface for a moment for that brief gasping breath of air before plunging us under once again! The power and magnitude of the waves smash and churn us about to be left with a feeling of helplessness and hopelessness and situated in such great despair.

Such big moments of life are neither planned nor rehearsed as they typically come to our doorstep, kick down our door, and catch us unaware and off guard. This is why our theology is so important as we wrestle with a good God and yet the fallen state of our world and the brokenness of our lives that do not seem as they can coexist.

As Walterstorff continues his personal wrestling, he cries out,

> How is faith to endure, O God, when you allow all this scraping and tearing on us? You have allowed rivers of blood to flow, mountains of suffering to pile up, sobs to become humanity's song—all without lifting a finger that we could see. You have allowed bonds of love beyond number to be painfully snapped. If you have not abandoned us, explain yourself.[56]

Unthinkable Loss

The questions linger and press in: How does one cope? Where does one turn? Can I find this courage you speak of to go on living? Will this empty void I feel ever be filled? Vividly I recall dear friends having to bury their three-year-old son after he drowned in a pool while they were away on vacation. While his parents were able to express that this little boy's life, though brief, was complete in God's eyes, the pain still remained. Weeks later the mother shared how she would daily go to his gravesite and, in deep anguish and grief, cast herself prostrate upon the newly churned ground above his casket to be close to her buried, lifeless child. Oh, how deep the pain of searing loss!

Similarly, the memory of the heaving and sobbing of a close friend and father whose dear son chose to end his life suddenly with an intentional pull of a trigger still deeply grieves and saddens my heart. I loved that young man even as a son, for he was a former student I mentored for many years. I will never forget receiving that phone call that after six brief months of marriage he decided to remove himself from this earth. So many unanswered questions and so deep the hurt and pain!

In my calling as a school educator, I have had the unfortunate front-row seat to the wreckage of families torn apart and innocent children having to figure out why Mom and Dad no longer love each other or can't seem to get along anymore. Yet the expectation is that these, whom I will refer to as victims, must go on in life, do well in school, be socially adjusted with a half set of parents, and acclimate to their "new normal" ... as if they ever had a choice.

My heart breaks as I see young men and young women "masking up," having to put on a good face as they walk the halls of school, all the while knowing that, despite the external façade they attempt to wear, deep inside their hearts, they are breaking and the burden they carry is almost too much to bear.

Battle Zone

Yes, wars we study in history and the ones being fought today are horrific events. Over the last few years, ISIS has shown us the cruelty of the human heart through brutality on a massive scale. We have seen people killed in our inner-city streets and even men having their life choked out of them by those who profess to be keepers of the peace who stand for justice. All this seems just too much to be able to process.

But let's be clear that the day we were born, we entered a battle zone that is more intense than any war fought by man. It is one that does not require us to go to the local recruiter's station to sign up and register for the armed forces. Whether we like it or not, we are in a war. The question is, will we stand to, engage, fight the good fight, and trust in the providential hand of an almighty God!

Once the great deceiver succeeded in his surprise attack in the garden, he has been determined to be a thief and a murderer, set to kill and destroy. We should not be surprised at his presence and therefore should be prepared to be both on the offensive and defensive with God's Word as our constant guide.

A God Who Shares Suffering

For us to stand to with our masculine courage, we need to recalibrate our thinking about the King we serve, or we will wimp out and become a deserter. It is important to note that we do not serve a spineless, sanitized, weakened, wimpy, nonconfrontational, feminized Jesus. To embrace such a view will not prepare you for what lies before us, nor extract the good that does lie within us. We serve a battle-scarred Warrior King who experienced the effects of hell for us. Death couldn't stop Him, the grave couldn't hold Him, and the agonizing conditions He endured couldn't slow Him down. Give me any person in history to even come remotely close to accomplishing that!

I'll save the thinking time. You can't come up with anyone to fit that description! That is why "as early as the first century AD, the life, death, and resurrection of Jesus was being compared to a great military victory over a formidable enemy. This doctrine is called *Christus victor* (Latin for "Christ the Conqueror"), and for centuries it served as the primary framework for understanding Jesus' mission on earth."[57]

Where did this idea come from? In Jesus's own words recorded in John 16:33, "Take heart! I have overcome the world" (NIV). How did this happen? God turned His back on His Son (Matthew 27:46) and then crushed His Son (Isaiah 53:10) in an act of love for us so we might live through Him (1 John 4:9).

Who does such a thing?! If someone were to do a radical act of love to save one of my three sons from death and they were to live, I would vow my entire life of service to them out of a heart flowing with indescribable gratitude. How much more Christ the Conquering King did for us! He died to get us while we were yet sinners, and we get heaven as a result of what He did! His action on the cross declares that it is not what we must do, but what He did! Every other religion will demand we do something, but Jesus paid our debt in full! Wow! That is the King we serve and are called to follow!

Upon contemplating the nature and magnitude of what Christ did, Walterstorff, still wrestling with the loss of his son, writes these words (notice how he is working through this horrific loss),

> God is not only the God of the sufferers but the God who suffers. ... It is said of God that no one can behold his face and live. I always thought this meant that no one could see his splendor and live. A friend said perhaps it meant that no one could see his sorrow and live. Or perhaps his sorrow is splendor. ... Instead of explaining our suffering, God shares it.[58]

He continues by clarifying, "We strain to hear. But instead of hearing an answer we catch sight of God himself scraped and torn. Through our tears we see the tears of God."[59]

Active-Duty Warriors

While I have always deeply respected, admired, and even been enamored by our military and the various armed forces, I have never served a day in the United States military. However, as a follower of Christ, I have served many, many years following Christ the Conqueror. The battleground is all around us. Our front lines appear to constantly be pressing us backward, as our freedom and Christian liberties we have long enjoyed in America and other parts of the world are quickly giving way to a society more concerned about tolerance, political correctness, safe spaces, acceptance, and secularization. Christian principles and values are being questioned, censored, cancelled, minimized, rejected, and ignored. Instead of Christian warriors, more and more there are Chicken Littles that run in fright and cower in corners at the slightest hint of a fight. This doesn't cut it! Matthew 11:12 says, "the kingdom of heaven has been forcefully advancing, and forceful men lay hold of it!" (NIV).

John Henry Jowett in *Streams in the Desert* was completely spot on when he wrote,

> Evil never surrenders its grasp without a tremendous fight. We never arrive at any spiritual inheritance through the enjoyment of a picnic but always through the fierce conflicts of the battlefield. And it is the same in the deep recesses of the soul. Every human capacity that wins its spiritual freedom does so at the cost of blood. Satan is not given to flight by our courteous request. He completely blocks our way, and our progress must be recorded in blood and tears. We need to remember this, or else we will be held

responsible for the arrogance of misinterpretation. When we are born again, it is not into a soft and protected nursery but into the open countryside, where we actually draw our strength from the distress of the storm.[60]

We know as warriors of the cross of Christ that what we are called to do is to wrestle with the devil himself and then run. This is not just a run from the devil, but a run to our King of whom the devil has no power or authority over. The devil is not just against God and His people but against each one of them individually, and his attacks are intentional, focused, and aimed at breaking down individuals who claim Christ as Lord. Ephesians 6:12 is a call for us to step into the ring with the devil himself as we arm ourselves with the weapons of godly warfare.

William Gurnall is helpful here as he talks of how we must recognize that Satan hates us, accuses us, and tempts us. You must not, however, fail to see that God loves you, pardons you, and takes care of you. Gurnall writes, "The water from the town will do you no personal good unless you have a pipe that carries it to your own house."[61]

In other words, your strength does not come from yourself but from God and His Word. From the breath that fills your lungs to the boldness, courage, and intestinal fortitude, you must have to face your life giants looming over you. It all comes from Him, and we must stay connected to the living water and the true vine that offers life and vitality found in John 15:5, "I am the vine; you are the branches. Whoever abides in me and I in him, he it is that bears much fruit, for apart from me you can do nothing" (ESV).

As you recall the five-point summary from the creeds as well as your personal creed, find strength in the fact that you are a warrior designed with masculine courage. You do not beat the air but wrestle to win heaven and a permanent crown (1 Corinthians 9:25). Balance the focus on the next life while wrestling in this one. To meditate and delight daily on God's Word will be fuel to your inward fire and quicken your pace forward while repelling darts and pinning the great adversary to the wrestling mat. May God's courageous challenge of truth and for life found in Ephesians 6:13, "Therefore take up the whole armor of God, that you may be able to withstand in the evil day, and having done all, to stand firm" (ESV), be what defines your life, and when He calls you home to glory, might this be the posture in which you are found, standing firm on the high ground!

Courage Challenge

Please let me warn you. This courage challenge is not going to be an easy one, but you must take it on anyway. Here is the challenge: Recall a time or event in your life where you felt God was silent as you walked through a dark, lonely valley. You looked for relief, a different answer, a better outcome, and release from the pain and hurt, yet the response you wanted never came. To recall the moment, incident, or event and then extract and expose this from the recesses of your memory may require you to go back to a place you stuffed away into the forgotten corners of your mind because the dreadful pain in the memory has been too difficult to navigate. You may have figured out how to block, pretend, fake, and mask the hurt as if it never happened.

I challenge you to go there anyway and confront that event and the circumstances that surrounded it. I know firsthand that this hurts a great deal. The courage required is significant. It may be as one taking their fingernails and digging them into a big, ugly scab until the wound is exposed and ugly. It hurts like mad, but what you realize is that under that scab was dirt that was never cleaned out thoroughly, thus preventing good healing from ever taking place. This is your life! This is part of your story, and they both matter a great deal! If you do not go to this off-limits area at some point, it will haunt you and very likely will, in related circumstances going forward, have a crippling effect on your life or that of another.

Scars

For me, there was a time in my life where, through a variety of circumstances, God was calling me to not remain in my place of employment but to go. Where to, I did not know, but I couldn't remain where I was any longer. What followed was agonizing as I had to uproot my family from our community, church, school, and neighborhood that embodied everything we had grown to love deeply. We had moved there thinking this is where we would settle down for life, but why this plan? Why now?

I recall on several occasions walking out of my school to a back athletic field and just weeping during the last couple months prior to my departure. As I drove the large moving truck away from the community we loved, our departure felt like an exile and was a burden I carried for quite some time as the husband and father of three sons who all desired to remain. I know it pained my family and particularly my oldest son. It hurt my heart deeply to see and know he was hurting.

The Gift of Lament and Brokenness

I was able to relate to David when he writes to God in Psalm 56:8 "Record my lament; list my tears on your scroll—are they not in your record?" (NIV). To lament is to express deep passionate grief and sorrow. Lamenting is more than feeling sorry for one's self, but it encompasses pain, hurt, confusion, anger, betrayal, despair, and injustice. This can be just too much to bear! We see this in Psalm 88 where similar words are offered.

However, there is something different in Psalm 88. The darkness and apparent absence of God is the suffocating and helpless feeling one gets when reading this psalm. Unlike any other psalm, this one does not end with a hint of consolation or impending relief. Hear the cry of a lamenting and broken heart in these verses and notice the concluding thought in verse 18.

- I am like a man without strength (vs. 4).
- You have overwhelmed me with all your waves (vs. 7).
- You have taken me from my closest friends (vs. 8).
- I cry out to you for help, O Lord (vs. 13).
- Why, O Lord, do you reject me and hide your face from me? (vs. 14)
- You have taken my companions and loved ones from me; The darkness is my closest friend (vs. 18 NIV).

So what are we to do with our lament? Are we left to just put on a good smile and act as if everything is just fine? Shouldn't weakness or vulnerability be suppressed so our masculine courage can define us? After all, isn't that what men are supposed to do?

No! Brokenness and pain, while never something we ask for or choose, is something we are gifted to receive. Whoa! Come on now, a gift? Really? You have got to be kidding me. And why are we talking about brokenness?

No, I am not kidding. This is a gift, and I'll tell you why we are talking about brokenness amidst courage. Here is the deal: we are most courageous when we are broken as brokenness comes through falling off our throne, shame or humiliation, or an experience that simply unravels us. We didn't ask for it, but we surely experienced it! In this brokenness we have three options:

- We can run and avoid, as most do.
- We can pretend it didn't happen and keep trying to manipulate our circumstances and surroundings as we grasp to regain control through positioning and posturing.
- We can just simply be broken, knowing that the reality before you is true and that there is no need to run, hide, cover, and pretend but instead begin to lift our eyes up.

In the lifting of our head and eyes, we can then see the one who was lifted up not in his exalted and risen form, but the one lifted on a cross, broken, bruised, and crushed for me and you![62] Looking back at Psalm 88, one hint of hope is found in verse one where in his opening petition, David claims God's goodness by calling to him in the title, "O Lord, God of my salvation."

Hope is the writer's place of beginning! It is to say, "I am claiming your goodness, I know you can bring relief, and I know it can happen, even though I do not see it right now." A perfect God, removed and separated from human feelings or emotions, cannot identify with our sorrow and suffering. This is why His Son had to be sent to suffer, struggle, be crushed, and die so we might then taste redemption through the blood of His Son, Jesus Christ! In other words, He's been there and done that! This is why Jesus could say, "He that will lose his life, the same will find or save it."

The reality is that the true struggle has ended. Victory was won at the cross and in a vacated tomb. The question is whether we believe this or not and whether we believe this was done for us and our circumstances specifically. You see, brokenness is a God-initiated, God-induced, and God-ordained event to introduce us to ourselves and then to see our God in a way like we have never seen or experienced him before. On this side of glory, this is the norm, not the exception for the Christian warrior. We are not a cruise ship but a battleship; we must remember that the battle is short and the victory in Jesus is forever.

I understand that most of us are trained to take control and find success, satisfaction, and the thrill and adrenaline to come through for others because we can; yet to now "lay down our sword" leaves us feeling exposed and naked. However, this is where we must go. When we get to that point, there is one thing left to do, freely collapse in humble submission into the arms of a God who is constantly inviting, pursuing, and fighting for our redemption and full restoration through His crushed and yet resurrected Son! The plea of the lamenting and limping warrior and the good news response is found in the following two verses.

Psalm 51:8 (NIV) says, "Let me to hear joy and gladness; let the bones which you have broken rejoice." Psalm 34:18 (ESV) reads, "the Lord is near to the brokenhearted, and saves those who are crushed in spirit." Ah, what great words of encouragement! The God who draws near!

Even more, in 1 Peter 4:12–13, we read, "Beloved, do not be surprised at the fiery trial when it comes upon you to test you, as though something strange were happening to you. But rejoice insofar as you share Christ's sufferings, that you may also rejoice and be glad when His glory is revealed" (ESV).

Notice several things here. We are told not to be surprised. This is normal life for the Christian. Then we are told to rejoice and be glad as the suffering reveals we are found in Christ. We belong to Him. How do we know this? We are called His beloved! This is the vocabulary of heaven! It is the same word God used to describe His own Son when God spoke from heaven at Jesus's baptism.

Our Redemption Story

In conclusion, you know your circumstances and situation, but not nearly as well as He does. Sit on that for a moment. Rest in knowing that He knows! He knows! The Word became flesh and lived among us. He is working all things for our good and His glory. Though I never would wish to go through the circumstances I did some years ago, I can see God's guiding hand and how He, like with the children of Israel through the wilderness, was constantly guiding, directing, and never leaving my side. "For you, O Lord, have delivered my soul from death, my eyes from tears, my feet from stumbling, that I may walk before the Lord in the land of the living" (Psalm 116:8–9 NIV).

So live free today as you, with great hope and great trust, take your past memory/moment and bring it to the one who already knows and loves and paid the ultimate price. He is waiting to meet you in your greatest need as you begin a conversation with Him and those of significance He brings into your life for healing and restoration. If you are in the valley, begin to thank Him for how He is going to work this for good, for your specific good. Be patient! He is good and what He is doing is good! So thank Him now.

CHAPTER FIVE

FEAR CHASER

The LORD is a warrior; The LORD is His name.
—Exodus 15:3 (NAS)

*As we let our own light shine, we consciously give
other people permission to do the same.
As we are liberated from our fear, our presence
automatically liberates others.*[63]
—Marianne Williamson

Stand Your Ground ... Charge If You Must

One day on the plains of Africa, a young buffalo named Walter approached his dad and asked him if there were anything that he should be afraid of.

"Only lions, my son," his dad responded.

"Oh yes, I've heard about lions. If I ever see one, I'll turn and run as fast as I can," said Walter.

"No, that's the worst thing you can do," said the large male.

"Why? They are scary and will try to kill me."

The dad smiled and explained, "Walter, if you run away, the lions

58

will chase you and catch you. And when they do, they will jump on your unprotected back and bring you down."

"So what should I do?" asked Walter.

"If you ever see a lion, stand your ground to show him that you're not afraid. If he doesn't move away, show him your sharp horns and stomp the ground with your hooves. If that doesn't work, move slowly toward him. If that doesn't work, charge him and hit him with everything you've got!"

"That's crazy, I'll be too scared to do that. What if he attacks me back?" said the startled young buffalo.

"Look around, Walter. What do you see?"

Walter looked around at the rest of his herd. There were about two hundred massive beasts all armed with sharp horns and huge shoulders.

"If ever you're afraid, know that we are here. If you panic and run from your fears, we can't save you, but if you charge toward them, we'll be right behind you."

The young buffalo breathed deeply and nodded. "Thanks, Dad, I think I understand."[64]

We all want to be the lion who is not afraid of anything. If only we could be the lion who everyone fears and backs down from no one. I think of the world stage and how countries, much like the animal world, measure their power by the type of military and weapons they possess.

Ranked #1

In 2019, 106 world military powers were considered for the top ranking of the best global firepower. The ranking was based on each nation's potential conventional war-making capabilities across land, air, and sea. (Nuclear weapons were not taken into consideration.) The ranking was built on a formula using fifty different factors compiled and measured against nations.

In the end, it was concluded that the United States held the top seat for the best global firepower, followed respectively by Russia, China, India, and the United Kingdom, with a $716-billion budget. (Russia is number two with a $44-billion budget.) The United States has 13,398 aircraft, including 5,760 helicopters in service, 19 aircraft carriers, 75 submarines, and 2.5 million active personnel. So it is understandable that we are ranked number one in the world.[65]

Nations depend upon their number of troops, industries to produce goods, and natural resources such as oil to be recognized as a world power. As I read about this ranking, I first found myself being impressed with the United States military. But then I wondered how silly God must view such things. We actually see God's response to nations that attempt to plot against Him. Psalm 2:2, 4 says, "The kings of the earth set themselves, and the rulers take counsel together against the LORD and against his Anointed … He who sits in the heavens laughs; the Lord holds them in derision" (ESV).

Our Warrior King

We serve a Warrior King who is a man of war constantly fighting for his people. Seeing that everything belongs to our Warrior King, the writer of Psalm 24:1 declares, "The earth is the Lord's, and everything in it, the world, and all who live in it" (NIV). We are clearly at a distinct advantage! As a result, I can confidently declare, "What then shall we say to these things? If God is for us, who can be against us?" (Romans 8:31 ESV).

Puritan William Gurnall writes, "The strength of the general in other hosts lies in his troops … but in the army of the saints, the strength of every saint, yea, of the whole host of saints, lies in the Lord of hosts."[66]

Just think for a moment how the natural world is subjected to our Warrior King and how He bends the elements to His sovereign will. When the disciples were paralyzed with fear because of the troubled sea, with authority Jesus rebuked the wind and said to the waves, "Quiet! Be still!" (Mark 4:30 NIV), and immediately it became completely calm. Fleeing Egypt, the Red Sea parted for the Israelites (Exodus 14:21). God moved time backward as a sign for King Hezekiah (Isaiah 38:7–8). The earth shook, and the sky suddenly became dark when Jesus was being crucified (Matthew 7:51). We could go on and on.

As a Christian warrior, you must believe that your victorious King fights daily on your behalf. 1 Samuel 2:9 says, "He will guard the feet of his saints, but the wicked shall be silenced in darkness. It is not by strength that one prevails. The adversaries of the Lord shall be broken in pieces; from heaven He will thunder against them" (NIV).

In 1 Samuel 2:10 (ESV), the Lord is quite explicit, "The adversaries of the Lord shall be broken to pieces; against them he will thunder in heaven. The Lord will judge the ends of the earth …"

Isaiah 42:13 continues to emphasize the nature of this Warrior King that does not watch from the sidelines but instead leads the charge from the front with a shout as a "mighty man" and as a "man of war," as Isaiah writes, "The Lord will march out like a mighty man, like a man of war he stirs up his zeal; he cries out, he shouts aloud, he shows himself mighty against his foes" (ESV). Did you catch that? I love that phrase that He will "stir up His zeal like a man of war!"

Understanding zeal to mean "great energy, enthusiasm, and passion for a worthy cause" makes this verse spring to life. Having had three sons in the house, I know what it means to stir up or agitate or initiate a conflict. Few evenings would pass without one of them bowing up to the other in a way to challenge and see where they stood in the pecking order. My youngest son, Jakob, always fought the hardest because he had to, and surprisingly he could hold his own. Here we see God being the initiator as he stirs up a fight with His and our enemies, and then Isaiah predicts the victory! The outcome is not in question. Victory is certain!

Don't Worry, Coach

My first year of coaching high school soccer, we were in the regional final to go to the state finals, and the game was tied after regulation, overtime, and sudden death, so we were going to penalty kicks. Each team had its five best players kick. It came down to our goalkeeper to make a monster save to go to the fifth shooter. If he didn't save the shot, we would lose. Despite the shooter's clear advantage, our goalkeeper saved the kick. However, in those days, the goalkeeper couldn't move until after the shot was taken, so it was called off, and the shooter had another chance to take the penalty shot.

I remember very well being upset at the ruling. However, before the kick was taken, our goalie, Ben Maynard, shouted to me as I stood at half field, "Don't worry, Coach! I'll save the next one!"

What? Serious? Who is so bold as to actually call this out before the kick was even taken? Well, on that day, he not only called it but actually did the unimaginable and saved the next shot, pushing us to the state finals, where we ended up winning the state championship!

For this young man, maybe that was a once-in-a-lifetime situation, but with God, we see Him saying over and over, "I got you! This is going to be fine. You are on the winning side! Take heart, stand to, and have courage! Go for it!"

So why fear when we know the wicked will be silenced and lose as God will, in His words, *break them in pieces*?

Running with Us

As a high school senior at the boarding school I attended, our soccer coach told us that we were going to get up at 6:00 a.m. and run three miles every morning. Unlike most coaches, he would run it with us. The catch was that as soon as one of us beat him on this three-mile run, then we would not have to do the run any longer. The coach the year before rode his motorcycle in front as all the players ran, but what this new guy said was a game-changer! He was actually going to run with us, and he was going to feel and experience everything we were … and maybe more as he pushed himself to the limit every morning.

In those days, I looked at him as the opposition. If one of us could only beat Coach, then we could be done with this crazy 6:00 a.m. running. That was my mission. On most mornings I would run right beside him in front of the pack. I was determined to make the last push and beat him at the finish line.

However, the last quarter mile was up a huge hill, and each morning, it felt like he was toying with me as he would kick it in and sprint up that hill, only for him to finish first time and time again. I remember players wishfully talking about how we could beat him, and we encouraged and even offered incentives if someone could beat him.

Finally, almost three weeks into this morning routine, my friend Phil, who was typically near the front every morning as well, was determined to make this the day he passed Coach. He stayed right beside him the entire way, and when they got to the final hill, where Coach usually accelerated past us, this time Phil kicked it into overdrive and exploded up that last hill, of course with us cheering him on until he reached the end of our run! We all thought Phil was a hero that day! Finally, he had won the prize and defeated Coach!

Looking back, all along it was our coach who was the hero—even after Phil passed him. Coach had become one of us. While we didn't see it this way at the moment, we actually desired to be like him. We wanted to be able to run the race with perseverance and endurance and to win! He brought the best out in us as we daily pressed to train harder and not give up as he offered himself as the standard to be followed.

To this day, I can remember Coach's response to losing when we all reached the finish line. With a smile on his face and an outstretched hand to Phil, he said, "Well done, Phil. You did it. I am proud of you," as we wildly cheered for Phil!

In my head, I was thinking, *Wait, Coach, you lost. Aren't you upset by your defeat?*

In reality, Coach never was defeated. All along his goal was that someone would actually pass him, but he modeled and set a high bar and was never going to make it easy or simple on us.

In the end, this was the best day for Coach. In fact, I would suspect that had none of us ever passed him, he might as well have been disappointed. He ran with us to motivate and challenge us, yet he never let us take the easy road in order to bring out the very best in us!

This story of my high school soccer coach gives us a little glimpse into what our King has done. He entered the messes of humanity and came to Bethlehem, yes, in a manager and as a baby, but with a sword drawn to fight sin and prepared to show the ultimate act of love by laying His life down for us! He experienced pain and deep sorrow and drank deeply of the cup of wrath God poured out for Him to drink in our place.

Yet He won at the cross as He defeated death, released captives from sin, and will have the final say when He returns and makes all things new! Yes, God laughs at the competition. He thunders and shouts as the man of war and puts a complete end to those who will attempt to rise up against His people. He is not just the historical King we read about in our Bible; nor is He just our future King victorious. He is our present-day Conquering King that goes before us in battle with the outcome predetermined and victory secure!

"But be assured today that the Lord your God is the one who goes across ahead of you like a devouring fire" (Deuteronomy 9:3 NIV). Whoa! That's my King!

Courage Challenge

You might be wondering, *So what does this all have to do with me?* Everything! As you will see drawn out in the next chapter, since we are made in His incredible image, we are purposefully designed to reflect the glory of God to others. However, before we talk about that, there is a challenge I need to put before you. The courage challenge for this chapter will require you to have conversations with yourself and God, and I challenge you to discuss it with others as well.

Here is it: Identify your three greatest fears and what causes them in your life. Why is this important? This challenge is intentionally sandwiched between talking about the nature of our King (this chapter) and how we are created in His image (next chapter). The fears you embrace will restrict and limit you from imaging the One who designed you and desperately desires for you to freely run a race, like my soccer coach, where our King is not removed and aloof, but instead is running beside you and desires to see you finish well across the finish line.

When my oldest son was a senior, we went on a high adventure father-son weeklong retreat in the northern mountains of California to a place called JH Ranch. As the week drew to a close, one of the fathers stood up and shared the following, "I have a confession to make; I hate heights! What I can't figure out is why on earth we can't worship God and grow in our relationship with Him without having to be suspended some thirty to forty feet in the air on all these high-risk elements!?"

While said with some joking, the fear he held was real, and yet he faced his fear by taking part in every high adventure element … and was glad he did so!

Confronted fears are liberating to where, like this man, one can stand in front of others and testify to conquering a fear that no longer was weighing him down and holding him back! However, the weight of fears not confessed, confronted, and conquered can be so heavy, burdensome, and debilitating that we can hardly think about them, let alone address them by walking straight through them.

Practically, it may mean you can hardly get out of bed in the morning. Instead we figure out the simple, no-risk, mundane, routine, meager tasks that allow us to limp to the weekend, only to repeat the same boring cycle over and over again. We were made for so much more than this! Come on! Let's go!

Our King engaged in our world and, in so doing, modeled how

He desires for us to "engage in the good struggle." Larry Crabb echoes these thoughts in his blog as he says,

> Until a man is humbled by acknowledging the fear that drives him, by admitting to an emptiness he cannot resolve, by realizing that the way he relates impacts no one deeply, and by bowing low in brokenness over how far short he falls from God's relational design for men, he will spend his life doing much that amounts to little.[67]

I am not sure what your fears are. For many men, there are some real, tangible fears. Am I going to make enough money? What should I do for a career? What if I don't get married? Am I getting old? Am I being or will I be a good dad or husband? Am I going to die? Will I or have I accomplished enough in my life? This list could go on and on.

However, it could be that there are deeper questions behind each of these. The Good Men Project speaks to three fears that many men face. While these fears are not gender-specific or life-threatening issues, they still can be terrifying to many men. The first fear is rejection, which often comes in the form of a job or relationship. This can land a heavy blow on men, leaving them feeling inferior and not capable of coming through as a man.

The second fear many men face is to be found to be irrelevant. In a performance-based world where we too often look to receive praise for what we do, we can suddenly be thrown into a downward spiral of despair by throwing up our hands, or we just try to work harder and longer in an attempt to become relevant again. Likely the most dangerous pathway in an attempt to be relevant again is to find someone else in a relationship who will suddenly affirm us as relevant or acceptable. The third common fear among men is for us to disappoint others because disappointment can put us on a pathway to irrelevance and ultimately rejection. For a man to feel he is constantly disappointing, he is no longer relevant, or his place of contribution in this world is minimal or to feel he has been rejected for what he has or has not done cuts to the very heart or essence of who men believe they are.

This wounding, left unaddressed, can cripple a man, sometimes for life. Whether you have experienced these fears or others, our fears do not have to be life sentences. Let me encourage you to, with all the masculine courage you can muster, apply the following opportunities as you uncover and examine your fears. Marianne Williamson, whom I quote at the start of this chapter, speaks in her poem entitled "Our Deepest Fear" of the personal freeing experience of being liberated from our fears and then as "we let our own light shine, we consciously give other people permission to do the same.[68] This witness and example encourages and inspires others to pursue this freeing and liberating experience for themselves.

1. Expose your fear and consider whether there is true validity to this fear or merely thoughts the devil is putting in your head to mess with you and minimize your effectiveness as a man of God. Be careful, as your thoughts can become truths in your mind. Are you letting yourself believe a truth or a lie? The Great Deceiver would love to remove you from the battlefield. So stand to and engage with this first challenge despite the discomfort.

2. Confront and challenge your fear. When it comes to fear, you have two choices: run to it or run from it. What's it going to be? If your heart starts beating faster, maybe wildly, it just might be because you are about to embark on a challenge that goes to your masculine strength. Go for it! You must move forward. To remain in the same place is just as good as stepping back or away from the fear. Lean into it now! This might be asking a girl to marry you, going to your first job interview, speaking up when a young woman's honor is on the line, or asserting yourself when there is no voice of moral integrity in a group discussion. Let me give an example: I have coached over six hundred varsity soccer games in my career. Recently my team was in the state championship match. This

marked the tenth time I have coached in the state finals, and as the match was about to begin, my heart was beating faster just like it did during my first state championship match back in 1993. There are times when I speak in public that my heart will start to beat a bit faster, even though I have done it countless times. This adrenaline, heart-pounding feeling is good. It means you are about to do something of significance, and as long as it is morally pleasing to God, this should not be viewed as a stop sign but an indicator that you are alive and well and living out of your God-design. In the end, you will be glad you pressed through and didn't turn around!

3. Speak words of affirmation to your own heart. I would suggest the memorization of Scripture. The Bible is loaded with great passages where we are both challenged to confront fear and to press through it in the strength of the Lord. I remember having a particular soccer player who, while he was an exceptionally skilled and gifted athlete, he would actually tell opponents things like, "I think you are better than me, or I am not sure I can beat you." This defeatist mentality hampered his ability to hit peak performance until this mental aspect of his game was addressed as we worked for him to first have victory over himself.

When little shepherd boy David went up against nine-foot-nine Goliath, he looked at him and shouted (which had to have made his heart pound), "You come against me with a sword and a spear and a javelin, but I come to you in the name of the LORD of hosts, the God of the armies of Israel, whom you have defied"

Yeah, take that, Goliath! But David isn't through. "This day the Lord will deliver you into my hand, and I will strike you down and cut off your head. And I will give the dead bodies of the host of the Philistines this day to the birds of the air and to the wild beasts of the earth, that all the earth may know that there is a God in Israel ... for the battle is the Lord's and he will give you into our hands" (1 Samuel 17:45–47 ESV).

Whoa! David wasn't messing around! He was naming it and claiming it, and then he went and did it in the strength of the Lord!

There are many other awesome scripture passages regarding the confronting and overcoming of fear. Here are some: 2 Timothy 1:7; Isaiah 41:10; 1 Peter 5:7; John 16:33; Psalm 27:1; Psalm 56:3–4; Romans 8:15; Romans 8:38–39; Psalm 27:3; 1 John 4:16–18; Joshua 1:9; Matthew 10:29–31; Deuteronomy 31:6; Psalm 23:4; Isaiah 35:4; Psalm 34:6; and Psalm 55:22.

Wait? Did you look up any of these verses? They are too good to just pass by! Stop and go get your Bible! I can promise you that to dwell on such passages and to commit them to memory will strengthen your heart and quicken your steps forward as a fear chaser!

Recall to mind and even write down the positive steps you have taken to confront your fears. These will serve you well as they will be stepping-stones for further courageous action forward.

David, before he set about decapitating Goliath, shared his successes with King Saul and others, just after we read in 1 Samuel 17 that "all the men of Israel, when they saw the man (Goliath), fled from him and were much afraid." David says, "Let no man's heart fail because of him. Your servant will go and fight with this Philistine (vs. 32 ESV). Your servant has struck down both lions and bears, and this uncircumcised Philistine shall be like one of them for he has defied the armies of the living God" (vs 36 ESV).

Notice how David drew on his past victories and connected them to his future situation? What victories has God allowed you to experience? Have a long-term memory when it comes to God's past faithfulness and high confidence and trust that He will be with you in your future circumstances as well! Too often we live life in a tunnel with blinders on, forgetting all that God has done for us. We are no different than the Israelites who were just brought through the Red Sea and then complained that they didn't have enough food … as if God were not going to take care of them!

Finally, stay focused on the present! Most of our fears have to do with the future and something we have not yet encountered. If we are not careful, we will write a sad, failed story ending before it even begins. You don't know the ending to your story so don't sell yourself and your God short. As President Theodore Roosevelt once stated, "At worst, if he (a man) fails, at least fails while daring greatly; so that his place shall never be with those cold and timid souls who know neither victory or defeat."[69]

Let me conclude this chapter by offering additional words from President Roosevelt, "A soft, easy life is not worth living; it impairs the fiber of brain and heart and muscle. We must dare to be great, and we must realize that greatness is the fruit and toil and sacrifice of high courage ... For us is the life of action, of strenuous performance of duty; let us live in the harness, striving mightily; let us rather run the risk of wearing out than rusting out."[70]

CHAPTER SIX

CREATED FOR THIS MOMENT

Let Us make man in our image, according to our likeness.
—GENESIS 1:26 (NIV)

We must be ready to allow ourselves to be interrupted by God.[71]
—DIETRICH BONHOEFFER, *LIFE TOGETHER*

A Close Resemblance

Growing up, there were two people I was constantly told I looked like. The first was basketball coach Steve Kerr of the NBA champion (2015, 2017) Golden State Warriors. This comparison first began when Kerr played for the Chicago Bulls, winning five NBA championships alongside Michael Jordan. Of course, after people saw me shoot a basketball, the comparison quickly went out the window!

The other comparison was to my father. It was very common for people to say in my younger years, "You look just like your father!" In fact, in my early twenties, we were often mistaken as brothers. However, it was an even greater compliment when someone stated that I acted like my father. The appearance I had almost nothing to do with, but my actions aligning with his meant that I was following not just in my father's footsteps but in the steps of Jesus, as my father's chief end was to be more like Christ! I respect and admire my father a great deal, so that always was a compliment to me.

However, what about the fact that Scripture tells us that we are like God? We see right away in Genesis where God, speaking to the Trinity, says, "Let us make man in our image …" (Genesis 1:26 NIV). Isaiah 44:24 removes any doubt that we are designed in our Creator's image, "Thus says the Lord, your Redeemer, who formed you from the womb, 'I, the Lord, am the maker of all things, Stretching out the heavens by Myself, And spreading out the earth all alone'" (NAS).

So He made us, and He made us like Him. Exodus 15:3 tells us, "The Lord is a warrior; the Lord is his name!" (NIV). When I consider these passages alongside the fact that the Hebrew root of the Latin phrase for "image of God" is *imago Dei*, which means image, shadow, or likeness of God, what we find is that we literally are a snapshot of God Himself.

Whoa! So what does that mean? First, it means that God has created us to reflect His characteristics of being creative, moral, relational, social, communicative, spiritual, intelligent, purposeful and much more.

Performance, Paychecks, and Popularity

This is integral to our discovery of what it means to live fully out of our masculine design. Fairly early in life, we unfortunately find our identity or lack thereof by those things we are able to do or not do well. The athlete becomes known as the jock, the smart guy who reads and studies and gets great grades becomes known as the nerd, and the guy who can't do either turns to humor to offset his inadequacies, shame, and embarrassment and quickly becomes known as the class clown.

As we move forward in life, men continue to find their identity in what they do, but it becomes more than that. As their competency grows, often so does their paycheck, which enables them to own certain things that can lead to establishing one's status in life. Along the way, who one knows and the circles they run in can determine if one is acceptable or not. So in summary, one's identity becomes wrapped up in these big three pursuits: competency, cash, and connections, or performance, paycheck, and popularity.

Here are the major flaws with this type of pursuit and living. Your competency and performance ticket is good for one day ... and typically one day only. Tomorrow that ticket is no good. You have to do it all over again. And who knows if the audience that you are performing for, whether it is a boss or a client, will find your achievements acceptable tomorrow. If you put your identity in performance and competency, you will live a restless life always proving, earning, and striving for the approval and acceptance of others!

Second, you will never have enough money as there will always be someone with more and someone possessing something that you wish you had. This, in the end, will leave you feeling wanting, lacking, and reaching for more.

Identify Source

As we talked about in our last chapter, the level of inadequacy and irrelevance will be disquieting to your soul as you are unable to come through for either self-imposed or fickle expectations of others in your life. A life where popularity and personal connections to others are tied to what you can do for them to keep your desired level of status will chain you to a performance- or works-based identity. If your primary audience is not Christ first and foremost, you will constantly be trying to create and recreate yourself based on other people. Who are you ultimately trying to please, and who have you given permission or power to determine your value and, subsequently, the possibility of devaluing you should you fall out of their graces?

If it is anyone other than the King himself, you are off course. The honest answer to this question may mean that you need to do a U-turn, return to the fork in the road, or recommit your life to listening and following after our Warrior King above anything or anyone else. Paul exhorts us "to put on the new self, created after the likeness of God in true righteousness and holiness" (Ephesians 4:24 ESV).

Thus the image spoken of is not an illusion but a reality that is renewed as we become more transformed (2 Corinthians 3:18) and start to take on the family traits handed down to us by our heavenly Father, our Warrior King. Wow! What a high and noble calling for us as men from where our identity has been forged!

Yet, if we think about the reality before us for a moment regarding the modern man, Monday through Friday has almost become a rite of passage one must endure to get to the glorious weekend where true living can now take place. For example, every fall, men across America flock to large-screen TVs to watch college football games with such fervor, passion, and enthusiasm that one would think their very existence depends upon the outcome of the game.

What if how we pursued all of life resembled the vigor, commitment, and dedication we display to athletics? When it comes to our work, we must remember that work was given to us in a state of perfection before the fall of man in the garden. "The Lord God took the man and put him in the garden of Eden to work it and keep it" (Genesis 2:15 ESV). A man who learns his trade and does his very best will develop a good name. It will not be long before his reputation proceeds him.

Instead of searching for work, jobs, advancements, and opportunities are often offered to him. "A good name is to be chosen rather than great riches" (Proverbs 22:1 ESV). Proverbs 22:29 adds, "Do you see a man skillful in his work? He will stand before kings; he will not stand before obscure men" (ESV). I have shared these ideas and verses with my sons for years and emphasized the value of a good name. Little did I know that while my oldest son was just finishing his junior year at Covenant College that he would be asked to apply for the director of high school ministry at the church where he not only had grown up as a young man but had also been volunteering with the youth for the last couple years. After a process of interviews, he was offered the job. Despite having one more year of college, he was hired to work part time until he finished his degree and could come on staff full time the following spring upon graduation.

As he called to share this news with me, I reminded him of these verses that speak of a good name and how his real interview was all the hours spent ministering to the youth while volunteering.

A man's name and reputation are in direct proportion to his willingness to work as if his employer is God himself, for in reality that is exactly the case. I believe, in more cases than not, how a man pursues those areas of difficulty or how he presses through adversity indicates how he pursues other areas of his life.

As a high school soccer coach, I tell my players that you can't turn it (effort) off in one area and it not affect other areas of your life. To grow lazy in the classroom will cause one to take shortcuts in a match when the going gets rigorous or extra effort is required in the closing minutes of the game. This is why Paul says in 1 Corinthians 10:31, "So, whether you eat or drink, or whatever you do, do it all to the glory of God" (NIV). This is comprehensive and for all of life!

In Proverbs 20:13, Solomon says, "Love not sleep, lest you come to poverty; open your eyes, and you will have plenty of bread" (ESV). This passage is not so much about sleep but the need for a strong work ethic. Ecclesiastes 9:10 puts it simply, "Whatever your hand finds to do, do it with all your might" (ESV).

This Is My Moment!

It is more than just fully grasping who we are, the development of a great name, and the need to throw our back into working hard. We must realize that God has placed us right here, right now, for this moment in time, culture, and history, and He has a plan for our lives specifically. We might look back with a forlorn look at the past, wishing for another time and place. However, just as Christ in His incarnation took on flesh for that specific long-awaiting moment, a moment that no one else at no other time could fulfill, we too, as His image-bearers, are called to live a full and robust life for the glory and advancement of Christ's kingdom right now.

We are not to flee or withdraw but to live and engage in the tension of a world that is broken and in need of men of courage who will engage in the redemptive process that God began and spoke of in Genesis 3:15 when we catch a glimpse of hope and a champion we can get behind and imitate. We see this in 2 Corinthians 5:17–21 where Paul speaks of us as being in the "ministry of reconciliation" (NIV). In a world that seems to be going mad with more conflict, confusion, and chaos, we are invited to offer our community a spirit of calm, a message of clarity, as we share the hope of Christ.

A Good Name

Men, it is critical for us to fully engage this next generation with a biblical world and life view in a world that is more and more hostile, opposed, and antagonistic toward a perspective that speaks of moral authoritative truth that lies outside of the individual person. Working with Christian high school students, I find how easy it is for them to accommodate, justify, and acquiesce to the trends and thinking of the day. This moment in time calls for us to not just push back or resist the culture but instead to be culture changers and shapers as we show and teach a broken and distorted world that there is truth, goodness, and righteousness that can be for them and that they no longer must walk in darkness but rather step into the glorious light offered through salvation in Jesus Christ. This is that very moment that we are created, designed, and purposed for.

Let's not miss it, men. An entire generation that follows behind is counting on us, even though they don't realize it. They need courageous men living out of their true masculinity fashioned after the Creator, our God and King! Let's not allow ourselves to become too big for ourselves.

Dietrich Bonhoeffer, a renowned Christian minister and seminary professor, was imprisoned during WWII and ultimately executed by the Nazis for his resistance to Hitler. Yet, in *Life Together*, he reminds us of the importance but also the gravity of the situation when he says,

> We must be ready to allow ourselves to be interrupted by God. God will be constantly crossing your paths and canceling our plans by sending us people with claims and petitions. We may pass them by, preoccupied with our more important tasks ... It is a strange fact that Christians and even ministers frequently consider their work so important and urgent that they will allow nothing to disturb them. They think they are doing God a service in this, but actually they are disdaining God's "crooked yet straight path."[72]

Men, there is nothing worse than arriving at the end of a day, year, career, or life, only to realize that you have squandered an opportunity that can never again be replayed, relived, rewound, or reclaimed. Despite the name given by your birth parents, may your heavenly Father's name for you be faithful, faithful now and faithful to the end! A good name can take a lifetime to build and a single event to destroy, and thus we are called to steward well the name we have. You will not regret it! The preacher in Ecclesiastes 7:1 says it beautifully, "A good name is better than precious ointment, and the day of death than the day of birth" (ESV).

As you wrestle with all this, consider that your name and reputation that depicts or defines your identity will be forged by the person you hold in highest regard. The one who affirms and validates gives you your marching orders. You might not even recognize this in your life, but this is a reality. Whoever sits on the highest pedestal in your life will be the shot-caller! Let this verse resonate in your entire being what the Creator of the Universe said about you! "We (YOU) are his workmanship, created in Christ Jesus for good works, which God prepared beforehand, that we (YOU) should walk in them" (Ephesians 2:10 ESV).

Do you comprehend what this means? We are His masterpiece, sculpted, chiseled, designed, and crafted uniquely, individually, and purposefully to do certain tasks (good works) that He, the Creator and King of the Universe, has given us the opportunity to perform for Him. When we do good things, our attitude should not be, "Whoa, did you just see what I did?" If it were good, it was good because God allowed you to do it and He ordained that specific task for you to do. In other words, you did what you were supposed to do, what you were designed and created to do! So when you do something well, in humble submission we can say, "Thank you for the opportunity to be in the King's service. I am so incredibly humbled and honored to be counted as one of the King's men!"

May our lives be an offering that reflects the message found in Romans 12:1, "Therefore, I urge you brothers (and sisters), in view of God's mercy, to present your bodies as a living sacrifice, holy and acceptable to God, which is your spiritual act of worship" (ESV). The King James Version refers to this as your "reasonable service." In other words, God is saying this is not an unreasonable request because these tasks have been prepared for you to do right now at this moment. This is precisely what you were made to do. Now go and do it! And may you feel God's pleasure as your King as you courageously live in His presence. Coram deo!

Courage Challenge

To attempt this challenge will require you to have several people in your life who know you well enough to both evaluate your life and offer you direct and honest feedback and accountability for your life for the following questions:

1. Get the conversation started by asking a close friend to respond to some of these questions:
   - How would you describe me?
   - What is the word on the street about me?
   - If my name were to be brought up at a dinner party, what are the words people would be using in reference to me?
   - Am I faithfully stewarding my God-given gifts and abilities?
   - In an unbelieving world, am I living with integrity where my name is impeccable to a world looking for an excuse to cast blame or fault with Christians?
   - What would people say about me at my funeral if I were to die today?

2. Tell me the top three ways that you see me imaging God. Be specific. This is an important starting place for each of us. While the second question is going to be more difficult, I hope to hear words of affirmation that will be an encouragement of things to continue.

3. Tell me of at least three ways where I fail to image God well. Be specific. Your friends need to be honest. True friends can offer words that on the surface may feel hurtful, but as Proverbs 27:6 says, "Faithful are the wounds of a friend" (ESV). In other words, a true friend offers words of redirection and correction in order to assist in getting a friend back on track.

4. Finally, based on what by your friends have shared, describe the specific ways you will set about to image God in a way where you begin to resemble Him more each day. I would encourage you to begin declarative sentences with "I will" statements or "I commit to resemble or image God by ..."

CHAPTER SEVEN

THE UNCOMPROMISED WAY

Thus says the LORD: "Stand by the roads, and look,
and ask for the ancient paths, where the good way is;
and walk in it, and find rest for your souls."
—JEREMIAH 6:16 (ESV)

In reading the lives of great men, I found that the first victory they
won was over themselves ... self discipline with all of them came first.[73]
—PRESIDENT HARRY S. TRUMAN

Ready, Fire, Aim

The latest, greatest, quickest, fastest, newest thing can quickly captivate our emotions, attract our attention, allure our senses, seduce our fascinations, and entice our temptations. This is the age we now live in. There is no time to reflect, ponder, consider, muse, contemplate, or meditate as one might miss an opportunity to get ahead or at least to maintain status quo with societal expectations and norms. So forward not back, progressive not reflective, or new not old is the thinking of the day because perceived primitive thinking, values, and principles will hold one back from modern, innovative, and dynamic viewpoints for living. Phew! Are you tired yet? But wait. It doesn't have to be that way.

Look at this passage from Jeremiah 6:16, "Thus says the LORD: 'Stand by the roads, and look, and ask for the ancient paths, where the good way is; and walk in it, and find rest for your souls'" (ESV). Here we are told to stand, look, and ask! Who does that anymore? After all, we have our iPhone that can tell us in a moment's notice everything we need! In a "ready, fire, aim" world, this passage is disquieting to the soul, for this takes patience and requires one to stop and question, examine, and deeply and thoroughly investigate the current realities. Yet the command persists even in a frenzied world despite satisfaction being elusive and brief and momentary happiness being tied to cheap thrills, quick jolts, and fixes of pleasure. We are told to stop and find that ancient path, the good way to find true rest for our souls.

Walk This Way

Isn't it something that the secret to life is hidden right in this passage like a buried treasure to be discovered? Interestingly enough, there is nothing that must be built, created, developed, or manufactured. Instead it is a return to the past, something that has been there all along! The Lord says this, "Ask for the ancient paths ... to find rest for your souls!" How similar to the Savior's invitation "Come to me ... and I will give you rest" (Matthew 11:28 NIV).

In Isaiah 30:21, we see the Lord wanting to be gracious to a rebellious people that turns and returns to these ancient paths of following after him when he says, "And your ears shall hear a voice behind you, saying, 'This is the way; walk in it'" (NIV) when you turn to the right or left. He promises to guide us and then provide rest as we walk in the good way. Isn't that something we all want? We labor hard each day, week, year, and lifetime and are always looking forward to a rest from our labor.

But maybe it is not so much the actual work from which our

bodies crave physical rest as it is a rest for our souls, rest that offers peace, a quiet heart, and a satisfied spirit. How does this happen? This happens when we are walking in the good way, where we seek His face and do everything for the glory of God. When I do this, it is no longer about sleep-deprived, anxious nights, but where I can put my head on my pillow at night and know I am following Christ, offering Him my first-fruits, and can then leave the results and outcomes to him. Psalms 17:5 offers a promise to following these ancient paths, "My steps have held fast to your paths; my feet have not slipped" (ESV).

In essence, we see God saying here, "Follow me! I got you. You are on a good path. I will not let you slip, stumble, or err on this journey. I know the way you should be going, and I will lead you well."

Longs Peak, Colorado

During the summer of 2017, my family was spending a week's vacation in Colorado hiking, backpacking, and taking in the beauty of God's creation found in the Rocky Mountain National Forest. My oldest son and I wanted to hike Longs Peak, one of the 14,000-foot-high mountains in Colorado. As we were talking to expert mountaineers about this hike, they were explaining the dangers of it, saying that two weeks ago, even though it was already June, they had received four feet of snow on that particular mountain. They shared that a portion of the trail was very dangerous, as one must navigate the rock field where the path is only about two feet wide, and to slip there is sure death, as the drop is about 150 straight down at that point.

He continued by saying we would need spikes and snowshoes and would need to depart at two in the morning in order to reach the summit and have time for the descent. He added that already this spring three climbers had slipped off the ledge to their death. While we both are up for a good challenge, not afraid of a little risk, I quickly concluded that this was not the adventure that we were going to be taking part in because the risk exceeded the thrill.

Of course, my twenty-year-old invincible son said, as soon as we exited the mountain climbing shop, "You know, Dad, we really should do that. And if it doesn't work out for us and we fall, well, you know, we all have to go sometime."

The wiser, older man made the decision for the both of us on that day.

As you read this, you may be saying to yourself, "Well, of course you shouldn't have gone down that path. That would have been foolish, even if all the snow had melted." However, how many times have you or others you've known gone down a path with little regard to where that path may lead? It doesn't take long before we find ourselves in a situation that we believe we are past the point of no return. I would imagine that as those three young men were attempting to cross that slippery rock field, they all thought at some point, *If we can just get to the other side and pass this dangerous part of the trail, we will be fine.*

Navigating the Rock Fields

It is interesting how this passage in Jeremiah develops. Up to this point, we see the formula for navigating through the rock field, so to speak, and even assurance later on that God promises He will be right behind us, telling us which way to go. What does that look like? It is for the Holy Spirit to guide, direct, convict, and lead us down the good path. God gives these commands. Remember what you learned as a child, "The Lord is my Shepherd, he leads me ..." For this Jeremiah passage, look at these keywords:

1. Stand. Stop all this frenetic running around. Just stop right there and stand still! Quite all that commotion. How often do we act like a frenzied swimmer in the ocean as if a shark is approaching?

2. Look. As you stand there, you will be able to actually evaluate and critique the path before you and then determine the best direction to either continue running in or where you might need to pivot and make a change of direction.

3. Ask. Don't try to just figure this out on your own. Seek good counsel from others. Talk to those who have gone before, those who are on the path you believe God is calling you down. Allow others to redirect the trajectory you are on if it is not the good way. Just like when my son Josh and I were considering the idea of climbing Longs Peak, we didn't just charge into it uninformed. No, we went to the experts to ask their professional opinion. We got help!

4. Walk. Get moving in the right direction as you head toward the good way. He then says that when we do these things, He promises to be with us every step of the way, talking in your ear, telling you which way to go. However, here is the kicker in all this. Just after God gave the formula for the good way, we get the Israelites' response, "We will not walk in it." I read this, and I am thinking to myself, *You have got to be kidding me!*

Running Blindfolded

This would be the equivalent of a person being blindfolded in a forest and the person who blindfolded them saying, "Stop! Do not take another step forward without listening to my voice. There are rocks to fall on and roots to trip you up. There are drop-offs and ledges where you can really mess yourself up if you fall off. Just listen to me, and I will safely guide you down the mountain."

Can you imagine if your blinded partner shockingly replies, "Nah, I'm good. I got this. I don't need your help. Just leave me alone and I will navigate my blindfolded self successfully down this mountain without any help from you."

Can you imagine this? How ridiculous it would be to say this!

Trail Guide

On one of the family hikes during the 2017 summer in the Rocky Mountains, we came upon an older gentleman who had a young man tightly grasping his arm. The twenty-something man was blind and used a long ski pole for support and guidance as the two of them hiked up the trails they were descending. The older man was constantly talking to him in his ear. I was amazed!

He was saying, "Rock up left, root up right, walk straight, turn left ..."

Every step that young blind man was taking was completely dependent upon the older man guiding him. Mind you, this was not a casual walk around a park. At that point, we were already over 10,000-feet elevation, and they had to navigate some treacherous terrain. That picture caused this passage to leap to life. There were drop-offs, raging waterfalls, snow-covered paths, and every other obstacle one could encounter on such a hike.

I think you get the point. May our attitude not be like the children of Israel who, after being offered a sweet deal, turned up their noses and defiantly said, "NO!" Might our spirit be humble, willing, submissive, and much more like the young, blind hiker who literally relied on a command from the older gentleman to provide him words of advice for every single step he had to take.

Only If You Go With Us!

In Exodus 33, after the golden calf incident, God visited Moses to tell him that it was time to move on. God explained to Moses that He would give them the land of Canaan, as He had promised, but Moses was not going to be going with them. Moses pleaded with the Lord and said in verses 15–16,

If your presence will not go with me, do not bring us up from here. For how shall it be known that I have found favor in your sight, I and your people? Is it not in your going with us, so that we are distinct, I and your people, from every other people on the face of the earth? (ESV).

Do you hear the difference in the Jeremiah and Exodus passages? In Jeremiah, the children of Israel had concluded, "We not only don't need your help, but we don't want your help. We will not follow what you said." However, in Exodus, Moses was so dependent upon God that he said, "If you don't go with us, then please don't make us leave this place. We want to be where you are. In fact, without your presence, who are we? You are our identity. You are what separates us from all the other nations. We are in desperate need of your presence!"

God's reply to Moses in verse 17 was, "This very thing that you have spoken I will do, for you have found favor in my sight, and I know you by name" (ESV). What an amazing discourse between God and Moses and what a testimony to Moses where God told Moses, "What you have asked, what you are doing is pleasing to me … and considering the fact that I know you by name. In other words, we have a relationship with each other. I know you!"

Courage Challenge

To take up this challenge is to actually embrace a practice that would be quite counter to our nature as men. Of course we have GPS in our phones now, but before that, how long would it take you to actually stop and ask for directions if lost? Be honest.

For me, as long as I was still driving, it felt as though I was making progress, but usually was just as lost as from the first moment I felt I had lost my way. Maybe a better example is when we have a project where we have to put something together. How far will you go trying to just wing it until you finally pull out the directions, take apart what you attempted to do on your own, and then begin to rebuild and reconstruct, but now correctly, according to the instructions provided?

Yes, like in both of these scenarios, this courage challenge will require you to stop and ask for assistance from the Lord and others to determine if you are actually going in the wrong direction. As you do this, think of the example we see with Moses where God relents, and because of his relationship with Moses and Moses' correct response before God, we see God honoring Moses' request. In the same way, use the following three passages to determine whether you are on the good path or not:

1. "God is light; and in him is no darkness at all. If we say we have fellowship with him while we walk in darkness, we lie and do not practice the truth. But if we walk in the light, as he is in the light, we have fellowship with one another and the blood of Jesus his Son cleanses us from all sins" (1 John 1:5–7 ESV).
2. "I am the light of the world. Whoever follows me will never walk in darkness, but will have the light of life" (John 8:12 NIV).
3. "If you hold to my teachings, you are really my disciples" (John 8:31 NIV).

To have fellowship with God means you are following Him and are on the good path as you follow His teachings. As you stand and look, ask God to reveal to you areas in your life where you are not in fellowship with him.

Again, as you dive in here, you really need another person who knows you well who can shoot straight with you, who can experience a period of honest reflection, and who is willing to bounce thoughts off each other and just be honest together. Let's dig in!

1. Every one of us is on a journey. Stop and evaluate where you currently are on this journey you are walking down. Take a look back and consider the last three or four major decisions

you were forced to make: decisions that were not easy, decisions that were made under fire, and decisions enveloped in conflict and some emotion. Which of the following would best characterize the path you are currently on based on the most recent big decisions you have made:

- Unswerving, steady, climbing to higher ground (still on a good path)
- Erratic and undisciplined; at times off-roading and going rogue
- The path of least resistance, filled with compromising and little to no resistance, for sin is an open door for all who wish to travel on its path

2. For the sake of clarity, what were those decisions, and what made them difficult? Summarize the scenario, the decision you made, and how you arrived at that conclusion.

3. Based on how you answered question number one, plot out the trajectory you are on, should you make similar decisions. To make similar decisions as you have been, describe the path you would be walking down.

4. The goal is for our testimony to be, as is recorded in Psalm 17:5, which says, "My steps have held fast to your paths; my feet have not slipped" (ESV). What needs to change or be adjusted in your life so you either continue to make solid or better decisions so your life will clearly be marked as one traveling down what Jeremiah calls the good way? Start walking in those ways and you will forever be glad that you did!

CHAPTER EIGHT

MAN UP!

Be watchful, stand firm in the faith, act like men, be strong. Let all that you do, be done in love."
—1 CORINTHIANS 16:13–14 (ESV)

You can't measure manhood with a tape line around his biceps.[74]
—BILLY SUNDAY

Act Like a Man

Very likely, most of us have been told at one point or another to man up by either our father, coach, teacher, or friend. On the surface level, that sounds like a manly thing to say, but in reality, when we heard those words, few of us really understood what it meant and what was supposed to be our response. In fact, if asked to explain what those who said it meant by it, likely you would get responses that sound something like, "I just need to work harder" or "I need to not be a chicken and stop complaining."

Usually it was said not so much to inspire, but to caution that we were acting or looking like a wimp. However, when I came across this verse in 1 Corinthians, I nearly said out loud, "Wow, there is it!

The Bible actually describes in detail in a four-step plan how to man up!" Amazing!

We see in this one verse that four commands describe how one is to act like a man. However, before talking about the four commands, there is an important word that Paul uses that we should not skip over. We need to discuss what it means to act. Why is this word important? Back in the garden, it was a word that the entire human race wishes that Adam had understood and heeded. Adam did not act; instead he went passive.

In Genesis 3:1–7, Adam's help-mate wife was in a dialogue with the serpent, Satan, which is always a bad sign. When a snake starts talking and you are having a conversation with a talking snake, that should have been a sign right there of a serious problem. However, while engaged in this dialogue, Adam never once entered into the conversation, not with the serpent, not with Eve, not a word. Instead he passively stood by listening in as Satan craftily worked to convince Eve that God was holding out on them, that they really didn't need God, and if they would just eat from the tree they were forbidden to eat from, their eyes would be open, and they would be like God.

All the while, Adam did nothing! He went completely passive, and yes, our first father was completely gutless, lacking any sense of courage. The only time he acted was when he took part in the fall of humankind by eating the forbidden fruit as well. Seriously! Check it out for yourself in Genesis 3:1–7. To be a man requires us to be willing to make hard decisions, sometimes major life-altering choices.

Decision of a Lifetime

I am reminded that on 9/11, it was Dick Cheney in a bunker under the White House who had to make some incredibly hard decisions on the spot in the immediate hours following the strikes on the Twin Towers. Not knowing how many passenger jets had been weaponized by terrorists, the decision to take down United Flight 93 by our own

Air Force was ordered immediately. That became unnecessary as Todd Beamer and other heroes overtook the terrorists, and in the end, the plane crashed.

Consider those moments in your own life when you were faced with major decisions and were forced to act immediately and did or other times when you needed to act and yet chose not to. It is one thing to stand to and be ready to act, but then you can't just stand there. It is time to get moving! Reflecting on your action or lack thereof is helpful in understanding a bit more of your natural inclination.

Whether you face obstacles and charge headlong into the challenge before you or struggle to move an inch, the reality is that for you to be able to tackle the other four challenges in these two verses on being a man, it is critical that you are courageous in your pursuit of acting like a man. Let's take a look at each of these four commands that will require your actions.

Courage Command #1: Be Watchful

Let's not kid ourselves here. If you don't believe you are in the devil's crosshairs as he is taking aim for us, then you need to wake up. Attack is imminent! John Owen once wrote, "When we say a tree is firmly rooted, we do not say that the wind never blows upon it. The house that is built on the rock is not free from assaults and storms."

This is why Peter reminds us, "Be sober-minded; be watchful. Your adversary the devil prowls around like a roaring lion, seeking someone to devour" (1 Peter 5:8 ESV).

In Old Testament times, cities in Israel were fortified with walls of stone, but men were posted around the clock to watch for impending danger. We see a great example of this in Nehemiah 4:9 when the Israelites were working to rebuild the fallen walls of Jerusalem. They were being taunted and needed to be prepared for possible attack. Nehemiah 4:9 says, "And we prayed to our God and set a guard as a protection against them (enemies) day and night" (ESV).

A good soldier on watch, seeing the enemy emerge from the thicket, making his way towards the camp for a sneak attack, does not stand there and try to fight the battle on his own. Instead, he runs back into the camp to report to the commanding officer (in this case Christ the King) that the enemy is lurking outside the wall and appears ready to launch an attack. A courageous Christian soldier knows that Christ "(provides) the way of escape, that you may be able to endure it." "No temptation has overtaken you that is not common to man. God is faithful, and he will not let you be tempted beyond your ability, but with the temptation he will also provide the way of escape, that you may be able to endure it" (1 Corinthians 10:13 ESV).

He runs in the opposite direction of the possible attack. He engages in a dialogue with his commanding officer and seeks out reinforcements who can support the cause against the enemy. "Here he comes again! See, look over there! I can't do this, but you can! We are going to talk this out until the enemy simply retreats, knowing they've lost the battle!" This is why we are told to watch and pray! That prayer is the dialogue with our Commander!

This was the problem with Adam and Eve. They got into the wrong dialogue, not with God, but with Satan himself. Instead of running from the temptation, they drew toward the lure of the temptation until they had completely fallen and did each other no good. Neither pulled the other to higher ground and considered what God was thinking through it all.

Thankfully, our Commander, Christ Victorious, has also experienced temptation. Hebrews 2:18 tells us, "Because he himself suffered when he was tempted, he is able to help those that are being tempted" (NIV). As has been mentioned in previous chapters, we see in the garden of Gethsemane that Jesus is in a fierce struggle, pleading for God to "remove the cup of wrath" in going to the cross, while also willing to submit to His Father's will. Again, He modeled for us, in the greatest of temptations, how to overcome as He engaged in an intense dialogue with His Father.

As we look at Jesus's temptation to avoid the cross, what can we learn from this? Just as in Jesus's case, the devil will attack us at our greatest area of weakness. If there were one thing Jesus did not want to do in all His humanity, it was to go to the cross.

Do you know what that one thing in your life is? What circumstances cause you to be most tempted? For many men, it is in the area of sexuality where pornography lies, steals, pollutes, belittles, and enslaves. Instead of sexual relations confined to a man and woman's union in marriage that is grounded in love, freely shared in a lifetime commitment of faith and trust, it turns to undeserved, unearned, unholy, illegitimate pleasure with no purpose. You must run! For once you acquiesce to the sin, the devil starts shifting into high gear until you are addicted, numb, demoralized, and desensitized. He drops the pellet gun and picks up the rocket launcher aimed at destroying you.

Paul offers us a good warning in 1 Corinthians 10:12 when he says, "So, if you think you are standing firm, be careful that you do not fall" (NIV). Should we really be on that intense of a watch? Absolutely! Genesis 4:7 says, "Sin is crouching at your door; it desires to have you, but you must master it!" (NIV).

Attacks are eminent, the onslaught of the adversary is intense, and the lure and pull to drag you down will be with such force that it can only be countered with an intense conversation with the only one who has never given in to the serpent's cunning and crafty ways but instead demanded, "Be gone, Satan!" (Matthew 4:10 ESV).

By now, some of you might not be feeling so much like a warrior any longer but instead are feeling exposed on the open battlefield with no weapons and no armor for protection. Let me encourage you in three ways:

1. Confession: "If we confess our sins, he is faithful and just to forgive us our sins and to cleanse us from all unrighteousness!" (1 John 1:9 ESV).
2. Resistance: "Submit yourselves therefore to God. Resist the devil, and he will flee from you" (James 4:7 ESV).
3. Alertness and focus: "You are all sons of the light and sons of the day. We do not belong to the night or to the darkness. So

then, let us not be like others who are asleep, but let us be alert and self-controlled" (1 Thessalonians 5:5–6 NIV).

Jesus tells the adulterous woman at the well these life-giving words that changed her forever and are freely offered to us today: "Whoever drinks the water I give him will never thirst. Indeed, the water I give him will become in them a spring of water welling up to eternal life" (John 4:14 NIV).

In 2 Corinthians 5:17, Paul writes, "Therefore, if anyone is in Christ, he is a new creation; the old has gone, the new has come!" (NIV). Jesus continues to renew our hearts and fills and satisfy us in ways no other is able. So strap on that armor, pick up that sword, and prepare to do battle once again! This is why we are told to be watchful!

Courage Command #2: Stand Firm in the Faith

Paul points out in our theme passage that there is a location for where we should be standing firm. We are to stand firm in the faith. Why is this important? In Ephesians 4:14, Paul essentially is saying we need to straighten our spines and not be weak and willing to give in to just anyone or anything someone has to say as he writes, "So that we may no longer be children, tossed to and fro by the waves and carried about by every wind of doctrine, by human cunning, by craftiness in deceitful schemes" (Ephesians 4:14 ESV). Instead, we are to "destroy arguments and every lofty opinion raised against the knowledge of God, and take every thought captive to obey Christ" (2 Corinthians 10:5 ESV).

However, this is not going to come easy. You are going to have to fight for this every single day. Jude writes in verse 3, "Beloved, although I was very eager to write to you about our common salvation, I found it necessary to write appealing to you to contend for the faith that was once for all delivered to the saints" (ESV).

He is saying that even though you are a Christian, you are going to have to contend or fight and struggle with this every day. It's time to dig your cleats into the turf, lean in, and push back! This contending and struggling is a good thing. In fact, look at how Paul refers to this fight as his life is drawing to a close. He says, "I have fought the good fight, I have finished the race, I have kept the faith" (2 Timothy 4:7 ESV).

To stand firm and to contend for the faith requires you to have unwavering principles, values, and morals. I am reminded of William Wallace in *Braveheart* who has been captured and ordered to swear his allegiance to the king. If he does, he would be shown a merciful death that would be quick as opposed to a slow, painful death where his life would be "purified by pain."

When the queen comes to him in prison to plead for him to swear his allegiance to the king, he tells her, "If I swear to him, then all that I am is dead already." As she keeps pleading with him to confess to avoid a painful death, he tells her, "All men die, but not all men truly live!"

Where in your life are you so principled and hold to such conviction that you are willing to have the same response as William Wallace did at the conclusion of *Braveheart*? If you find yourself dropping your head and being frustrated with your current response due to your past struggles, be encouraged and challenged with Paul's words in Philippians 3:13–14. I am "forgetting what lies behind and straining forward to what lies ahead. I press on toward the goal for the prize of the upward call of God in Christ Jesus" (ESV).

Consider these questions of reflection before moving on. When you think of the faith as you understand it, what do you find difficult to stand for? What does standing firm look like to you, and who could or has helped you to improve in standing or contending firmly in the faith? We obviously see Paul standing firm in Scripture. Do you have a modern-day Paul in your life who you can look to as a model of standing firm? If not, who might serve in this capacity to provide your courage and strength in this good fight?

Courage Command #3: Be Strong

Some years ago when our family transitioned to Birmingham, Alabama, and I took a new job as a high school principal and was moving into our new house, the athletic director and head football coach of the school arranged to have the football team show up at my house when the moving truck arrived to move us in. That was a sight to see! All of a sudden I could hear the rumble of these country boys' pickup trucks coming up the road, and these strong boys got out ready to help.

As we began to unpack, knowing we had a piano to move in, I asked the boys, "Okay, so which one of you is the strongest?"

That set off quite a debate as they talked about who could take what and who and how much weight each could bench-press. Then I asked them which was better: the offensive line or the defensive line. Well, that got them going again, but in the end, even the O-line conceded that the defensive line was stacked and a force to be reckoned with.

As I think of the Christian life, we have to always be on our guard, ready to play good defense because when we claim Christ as our Lord and Savior, the true struggle and war within begins. Paul, in Galatians 5:17, says, "For the desires of the flesh are against the Spirit, and the desires of the Spirit are against the flesh, for these are opposed to each other, to keep you from doing the things that you want to do" (ESV).

The lines are drawn, there are two distinct camps, and one cannot reside in both comfortably. Romans 8:7–8 mentions, "The mind that is set on the flesh is hostile to God … and cannot please God" (ESV). So what is the answer in how we might find and show true strength?

1. God's Word must be read, memorized, and utilized. It is your manual, playbook, handbook, and guidebook as you navigate through life. Examine each of these verses to serve as a source of courage and strength to you:

- King David, when on his deathbed and passing his kingdom on to his son Solomon, said these words, "Be strong, and show yourself a man, and keep the charge of the Lord your God, walking in his ways and keeping his statues, his commands, his rules, and his testimonies … that you may prosper in all that you do and wherever you turn" (1 Kings 2:2–3 ESV). Did you catch that? David is saying, "Son, you want to be strong and act like a man? Then get into God's Word. Know it, study it, follow it, and keep it, and you will be successful."
- Where did David get this idea from? In Psalm 121:2, David said, "My help (strength) comes from the Lord, the Maker of heaven and earth" (NIV).
- In Ephesians 6 when Paul is talking about fighting with the armor of God, he says in verse 10, "Finally, be strong in the Lord and in his mighty power" (NIV). Similarly Paul tells Timothy in 2 Timothy 2:1 to "Be strong in the grace that is in Christ Jesus" (NIV).
- In Psalm 119:9–11, a question is asked and answered, "How can a young man (or any man) keep his way pure (Or how does he stay strong)? By living according to your word. I seek you with all my heart; do not let me stray from your commands. I have hidden your word in my heart, that I might not sin against you" (NIV).
- "So, if you think you are standing firm (being strong), be careful that you don't fall! No temptation has overcome you except what is common to man. And God is faithful; he will not let you be tempted beyond what you can bear. But when you are tempted, he will also provide a way out so that you can stand up under it" (1 Corinthians 10:12–13 NIV). I committed these verses to memory as a young man, and it has served me well for many years.
- Be encouraged by the good word Paul received from the Lord when he was struggling with his own weaknesses, "My grace is sufficient for you, for My power is made

perfect in weakness" (2 Corinthians 12:9 NIV). There are a million ways to fall down, but there is only one way to stand back up, and that is in the strength of the Lord.

2. Develop a strong distaste for sin. Until sin becomes bitter, our Savior will not be sweet. If you find that you are struggling with sin, know this is a good thing. It is when sin is present and we cease to be troubled by the sin in our lives that we should be most concerned. The great struggle within should lead us to the cross where we can see our Savior more clearly and hear His voice more audibly! The Christian must keep struggling forward, knowing that the only day he can stop is when he takes his final life's breath and can see Jesus face-to-face. When we claim the cross of Christ, we will continue to see that grace is far more powerful and far greater than sin. When we see the bigness of our sin, the cross becomes even larger, for it covers our sin. It is then that our love for our Savior should be overwhelming for the price He paid on our behalf, and our response should be to seek to follow Him more closely in humble submission.

3. Remember that we fight from a position of approval, not for approval. In fact, in Romans 8:1, Paul says, "Therefore, there is now no condemnation for those who are in Christ Jesus" (NIV). We are not living to earn approval. We already have it if we are found to be in Christ! Too often we stumble and fall and guilt and shame envelopes us like a low-hanging fog that just does not seem to want to go away. Yet, if we understand that we operate from a position of victory, that the battle has already been won by our victorious King, and that we can focus on "Wonderful Savior" and not what a "wretched man" that I am, then we are free to stand in the power and strength of the Lord.

Command #4: Do Everything in Love

You might be wondering why, of all the things Paul would put in a list to challenge us in our manhood, he enters the word *love*. Actually this is not a novelty found in one or two passages in the Bible. In the Bible (NIV version), the word *love* is mentioned 574 times! Paul does not suggest we should love at certain times. Instead his words were, "Let all that you do be done in love" (1 Corinthians 16:14 ESV). That word *all* is pretty comprehensive!

As we talk of love in the context of manning up and showing courage, I will speak of love in the context of men acting as iron sharpening iron in the hopes of pulling each other to higher ground as they seek to bring out the very best in each other. In Proverbs 17:17, the writer says, "A friend loves at all times, and a brother is born for adversity" (ESV).

In other words, tough times are coming, but a good friend is made or born for such as these very moments. Stop for a moment and ask yourself: who are your three to four closest friends? Now ask yourself if you are loving them well. You might say that you are not sure what it really means to love well. In John 15:13, John says this in speaking of Jesus, "Greater love has no one than this, that someone lay down his life for his friends" (ESV).

Wow! What does that mean for you? Are you to lay down (give up) your life for your friends? While that would be an act of love for sure, it is important to see love as simply this, "I chose to put your life before my own. I chose to inconvenience my life to convenience yours." That might mean that you feel uncomfortable for the sake of doing the right thing. Ephesians 4:15 says we need to be "speaking the truth in love" (NIV) and then remember that in those moments "love never fails" (1 Corinthians 13:8 NIV). Proverbs 27: 5–6a says, "Better is open rebuke than hidden love. Faithful are the wounds of a friend" (ESV).

True love is when we will hold each other to a high and unyielding standard of what it means to act like men. Society has said for years that boys will be boys. Such a standard has been the dumbing down for guys for some time now. Instead, what guys should be aspiring to is that boys will become men and real men will act like men, as defined in the theme passage for this chapter where we are watchful, standing firm in the faith, and being strong (in the strength of the Lord) while loving others well. This happens in the company of other men and other boys aspiring to act like and be men! This was the whole purpose or meaning behind my first book, *We Became Men*. The hope is that after reading it, guys would be called to higher ground where they no longer desire to be and act like young boys, but act like men!

In that book, I actually dedicated a chapter to what such a true friendship between guys should look like. There I wrote,

> You will need friends who can keep you on the path when everything about you wants to take the easy way out … True friendship is not about convenience, good feelings, or the benefits you can get from it. Instead, true friendship means being there despite inconvenience, standing alongside when your first reaction is "I don't have the time," or helping when even an association with the person or issue does not put you in the best light. A true friend has a responsibility to "rejoice with those who rejoice, weep with those who weep" (Rom. 12:15 ESV). When you hurt, I hurt; when you win, I win; when tragedy strikes you, it also strikes me. True friendship is walking through the pain of life, softening blows by absorbing some of their effects whenever possible. [75]

Courage Challenge

- Be Watchful: Where in your life are you most vulnerable and prone to come under attack? It is vital to identify this area because you can guarantee that the devil is coming for you right there in that place of vulnerability. You likely know when, where, and how it happens. It is your weakness, your Achilles' heel, and the devil knows this. It is his back-door entry point into your body, heart, and mind. It is good to know this and to be a watchman, but it is another thing entirely to be able to resist or stop the devil from sneaking in the back door. Here is where the courage factor comes in. Know that you have to identify this. It is time to talk it out. Share it with someone who can ask you the hard questions, can poke and prod in your life, and will give an honest response. Have the courage to share and to ask, and to invite accountability. You will forever be glad that you did!

- Stand Firm in the Faith: When you think of the faith as you understand it, where do you find it difficult to remain standing? To stand when everyone else is sitting down is unnerving; yet this is what we are called to do. We are told to contend or fight in these areas. Don't go into battle alone. Here is where you must lean on a brother(s) for support. Share your struggle and ask for them to commit to pray to the Lord on your behalf for this particular area where your knees buckle and you struggle to find the strength and faith to stand. God is faithful and will meet you in the place of difficulty, opposition, and struggle.

- Be Strong: As already stated, you fight from a position of victory! You are more than conquerors through Him, Jesus the Risen and Conquering King. In looking at the Scripture passages listed, both Paul and King David knew they drew strength and courage from the Lord. I encourage you to commit one or more of these passages to memory so you can draw strength from recalling it during a time of need.

- Do All in Love: To love those who do kindness to us or show affirmation to what we do is not that difficult to love that type of person. However, consider those people in your life who are just plain difficult to deal with or who are maybe even oppositional to you. These too are whom the Lord has challenged us to love. In so doing, we show both courage and exhibit how a true man acts. So who is that in your life? Identify that person(s) and continually show love to them. It won't be easy, but in many cases, you will eventually find that their heart may soften and you may begin to find common ground to where some day, you both may be able to actually call one another friends, as Jesus refers to us. Make that your goal!

CHAPTER NINE

I'M IN—ALL IN

I looked for a man among them who would build up the wall and stand before me in the gap on behalf of the land, so that I would not have to destroy it; but I found none.
—EZEKIEL 22:30 (NIV)

Forbid it, Almighty God! I know not what course others may take; but as for me, give me liberty or give me death.
—PATRICK HENRY

Power of One

After being imprisoned in South Africa for twenty-seven years, Nelson Mandela had every reason to hold a grudge and fight back against those who had done such horrific things to his people and him, but instead he immediately set out to bring healing to a broken and divided nation. In fact, Nelson Mandela, as he was being released from prison, said to himself, "As I walked out the door toward the gate that would lead to my freedom, I knew if I didn't leave my bitterness and hatred behind, I'd still be in prison."[76] He was known to have said, "Forgiveness liberates the soul, it removes fear. That's why it's such a powerful weapon."[77]

Nelson Mandela went on to be an anti-apartheid activist and lawyer and eventually was elected in 1994 as the first Black president in South Africa, a position he held for the next six years. Here one man refused to allow his situation to hinder him from making a significant and historical difference in the life of an entire nation!

And yet, when you read this opening verse from Ezekiel when God says, "I looked for a man among them who would build up the wall and stand before me in the gap on behalf of the land, so I would not have to destroy it; but I found no one" (Ezekiel 22:30 NIV), does not your heart just drop when you read this verse? Don't you just want to yell, "Step up, rise up, get up, do something … just don't sit there doing nothing"?

Hold on! Let's step back and scan the horizon! Should we be surprised? After all, who is actually standing as described in 1 Kings 8:61, "Let your heart therefore be wholly true to the Lord our God?" (ESV). Today, instead of words like initiate, act, resolve, and commit to describe our posture and response to opposition or even needs around us, words like apathy, passivity, and disengagement more reflect our nature and habits while worthy causes desperately need us to stand to and engage.

Man of God

NFL linebacker Demario Davis walked to his locker following his New Orleans win over the Seattle Seahawks in late September 2019 to find a white envelope that upon opening it revealed that he was going to be docked $7,017 for a uniform violation.

Davis, a committed Christian, had a custom gold headband with the words "Man of God" in block letters for everyone to see. He had been wearing it all season thus far and was surprised at the fine for violating the NFL's rule from "wearing, displaying, or otherwise conveying personal messages" during gameday events. Once he realized he was in violation, he didn't wish to set a bad example of going against the policies of the NFL and chose not to wear it again. However, what happened next surprised him.

Not only did he get lots of mail supporting him, but fans began to show up wearing "Man of God" headbands to games, and the NFL received great criticism for fining Davis, to the point where in early October the NFL rescinded the fine.

Davis said, "Yeah, most times they don't overturn something like that, so I just like to think that was the power of God working behind the scenes, man."[78]

Davis could have left the matter alone at that point but then chose to donate the entire fine to St. Dominic Hospital in Jackson, Mississippi, where his mother once worked. He then began to sell these headbands for $25 apiece, and any money generated would also go to the hospital. Whole classes and schools in the New Orleans area began to wear "Man of God" headbands, and young children began to wear "Child of God" headbands as well. Within two months, $300,000 had been raised!

Davis was shocked at the response and said, "That's just the power of God, man—he takes negative situations and uses them for positives. You notice like, people in the Bible—God doesn't look for the best or the biggest; he looks for the person who has been counted out. God is the king of taking bad situations and turning that into a positive."[79]

Just Need One Bold Guy

In my role as a high school principal, I was recently talking with a group of teenage young men regarding a weekend underage drinking incident. As we discussed the details, I individually asked them, "At what point did you realize the steps you were taking were wrong?" Each young man admitted that very early on, they recognized they were in the wrong but failed to stop their actions or that of their friends.

I then asked each of them that if any one of them had stepped up and told the other guys to stop, if their buddies would have listened to them. Every single one of them believed that the rest would have listened, stopped, and not gone through with drinking the alcohol. Why is it that there are so few with courage, so few willing to say "I want to be all in," doing the right thing all the time?

After all, to know what is right is often fairly simple. Romans 2:15 could not be clearer about this, "They show that the work of the law is written on their hearts, while their conscience also bears witness, and their conflicting thoughts accuse or even excuse them …" (ESV). Yet it is an entirely other matter to have the courage or guts to stand up and do the right thing. To stand in the gap is frightening and can be very uncomfortable, so we minimize and excuse and just believe that someone else will do it.

There is a tale of such a group of people that goes like this:

> This is a story about four people named Everybody, Somebody, Anybody, and Nobody. There was an important job to be done, and Everybody was asked to do it. Everybody was sure Somebody would do it. Anybody could have done it, but Nobody did it. Somebody got angry about that because it was Everybody's job. Everybody thought Anybody could do it, but Nobody realized that Everybody wouldn't do it. It ended up that Everybody blamed Somebody when Nobody did what Anybody could have done.[80]

How often does this happen in life? And what a difference it would have made had just one of those somebodies stepped up and done what anyone could have done!

This can quickly be compounded when we allow self-interest groups, financial benefits, and others' opinions, mixed with our own fears, stop us from engaging in the difficult and uncomfortable. Before long, little subtleties, compromises, and justifications form in our minds until we have convinced ourselves of something other than the truth.

Quickly right and wrong become blurred together as murdering innocent children is called "pro-choice," sexual perversion is called "an alternate lifestyle," cheating is called "little white lies," and even gay marriage has hijacked the rainbow as their banner to symbolize their movement, despite it being what God used to mark His covenant promise to declare that He would not flood the earth again.

So then why do we study the Scripture, listen to sermons, join small groups, and so forth if we never are moved to take action? James 1:22–24 nails this point when he writes, "But be doers of the word, and not hearers only, deceiving yourselves. For if anyone is a hearer of the word and not a doer, he is like a man who looks intently at his natural face in a mirror. For he looks at himself and goes away and at once forgets what he was like" (ESV).

Just Mercy

Without a doubt, to stand up will mean you will stand out because very few are actually standing in the gap today. This is why when Bryan Stevenson, author of the book and movie *Just Mercy*, chose to leave his hometown of Baltimore, get his law degree from Harvard, and go to racially charged Montgomery in 1989 to offer legal counsel to inmates on death row despite no cases having been overturned yet in Alabama. It was not a popular choice, particularly for a Black man. However, the harassment, abuse, threats, and intimidation did not stop him from taking up many cases, including Walter McMillian's, and ultimately securing his freedom from death row after six long years for a crime he did not commit.

When Congress no longer funded Alabama's operation of the Southern Center for Human Rights (a death-penalty defense organization), he didn't let that slow him down. He went on to found the Equal Justice Initiative and guaranteed a defense of anyone in Alabama sentenced to the death penalty. This was quite an initiative as Alabama was the only state that did not provide legal assistance to people on death row and had the highest per capita rate of death penalty sentencing. By 2019, the EJI had saved 135 men from the death penalty who were wrongly accused. How such bold and courageous work must please the heart of God as Mr. Stevenson's work is reflective of Micah 6:8, "But he has shown you, O man, what is good; and what does the Lord require of you? To act justly, and to love mercy and to walk humbly with your God" (NIV).

What if Mr. Stevenson hadn't gone? What if he hadn't fought for Mr. McMillian? He likely would have received the electric chair, like the six men Mr. McMillian had become acquainted with during his six years in prison.

But what about you? What is the cost to remain indifferent, unmoved, and apathetic? The consequence for a nation of halfhearted men was dire in the days of Ezekiel. Are we any different today? We now are seeing the results of a nation filled with reclining "lazy boy" indifferent men. Just think for a moment of areas in our world, nation, local communities, churches, and families that are in great need for godly men to step forward. Have we ignored them, or have we just become indifferent and complacent? There must be a change for our nation, communities, and families in order to prosper!

The Fellowship of Christian Athletes (FCA) has a creed that is the epitome of being all-in. As you read this creed, could you imagine what a group of people, deeply committed to this creed, could actually accomplish for God's kingdom?

FCA, The Competitor's Creed

I am a Christian first and last.
I am created in the likeness of God Almighty to bring Him glory.
I am a member of Team Jesus Christ.
I wear the colors of the cross.

I am a Competitor now and forever.
I am made to strive, to strain, to stretch
and to succeed in the arena of competition.
I am a Christian Competitor
I face my challenger and as such, with the face of Christ.
I do not trust in myself.
I do not boast in my abilities or believe in my own strength.
I rely solely on the power of God.
I compete for the pleasure of my Heavenly Father,
the honor of Christ and the reputation of the Holy Spirit.
My attitude on and off the field is above reproach—
my conduct beyond criticism.
Whether I am preparing, practicing or playing;
I submit to God's authority and those He has put over me.
I respect my coaches, officials, teammates and competitors
out of respect for the Lord.
My body is the temple of Jesus Christ
I protect it from within and without.
Nothing enters my body that does not honor the Living God.
My sweat is an offering to my Master.
My soreness is a sacrifice to my Savior.
I give my all—all of the time.
I do not give up. I do not give in.
I do not give out. I am the Lord's warrior—
a competitor by conviction and a disciple of determination.
I am confident beyond reason because my confidence lies in Christ.
The results of my efforts must result in His glory.
LET THE COMPETITION BEGIN.
LET THE GLORY BE GOD'S.[81]

Wow! What a statement for not just athletes to follow but every Christian who bears the name of Christ in how we pursue life. As Christians we have already entered the race, laying "aside every weight, and the sin which clings so closely to us, and let us run with endurance the race that is set before us" (Hebrews 12:1 ESV) that we accomplish the goal of finishing well and receiving the reward of hearing, "Well done, good and faithful servant, ... enter into the joy of your Master" (Matthew 25:23 ESV).

For so many of us today, such a statement may seem too radical, too over-the-top enthusiastic. However, such enthusiasm and passion for life are not unheard of as men who are faced with overwhelming odds have stood unmovable, unshakable, and unfashionable in the face of such opposition.

Give Me Liberty or Give Me Death

Few speeches are more rousing than the one Patrick Henry delivered as the American colonists were discussing their liberation from the English. Patrick Henry gave this address on March 23, 1775, in hopes of raising a militia to put Virginia in a posture of defense. Here is an excerpt from his speech:

> They tell us, sir, that we are weak; unable to cope with so formidable an adversary. But when shall we be stronger? Will it be the next week, or the next year? Will it be when we are totally disarmed, and when a British guard shall be stationed in every house? Shall we gather strength by irresolution and inaction? Shall we acquire the means of effectual resistance, by lying supinely on our backs, and hugging the delusive phantom of hope, until our enemies shall have bound us hand and foot? Sir, we are not weak if we make a proper use of those means which the God of nature hath placed in our power. Three millions of people, armed in the holy cause of liberty, and in such a country as that which we possess, are invincible by any force which our enemy can send against us. Besides, sir, we shall not fight our battles alone. There is a just God who presides over the destinies of nations; and who will raise up friends

to fight our battles for us. The battle, sir, is not to the strong alone; it is to the vigilant, the active, the brave. Besides, sir, we have no election. If we were base enough to desire it, it is now too late to retire from the contest. There is no retreat but in submission and slavery! Our chains are forged! Their clanking may be heard on the plains of Boston! The war is inevitable²and let it come! I repeat it, sir, let it come. It is in vain, sir, to extenuate the matter. Gentlemen may cry, Peace, Peace but there is no peace. The war has actually begun! The next gale that sweeps from the north will bring to our ears the clash of resounding arms! Our brethren are already in the field! Why stand we here idle? What is it that gentlemen wish? What would they have? Is life so dear, or peace so sweet, as to be purchased at the price of chains and slavery? Forbid it, Almighty God! I know not what course others may take; but as for me, give me liberty or give me death![82]

Don't you hear the passion and enthusiasm in this moving and inspirational speech? If you were listening to Patrick Henry give this speech back in 1775, what would have been your response? What would invite such passion and inspiration in my life that would cause a similar response to Patrick Henry? Great WWII General George S. Patton once said, "The secret of victory lies not wholly in knowledge. It lurks invisible in that vitalizing spark, intangible, yet as evident as the lightning, the warrior soul!"[83]

Patton believed that there was something deeply special hidden inside of men that once that fire was lit and that passion was burning red-hot, there was little that could resist and stand in the way of the warrior soul that had bought into a cause greater than himself.

Save One More ... Just One More

Movies like James Bond 007, *Mission Impossible*, *Lord of the Rings*, *Star Wars*, and so forth are all engaging to watch, and of course the heroes and what they stand for are those we admire and respect. However, a particular movie, *Hacksaw Ridge*, caught my attention like few have been able to do so in recent years. The true story is about Desmond Doss, who entered the war as a conscientious objector. He refused to carry weapons but instead wanted to be a medic to help and save other people. For this stance, he was bullied, beaten by fellow soldiers, harassed, and abused, yet it was the love of his country and his faith in God that refused to allow him to quit.

In 1945, while attacking a ridge in Okinawa, Japan, he single-handedly saved seventy-five men as he dodged bullets and dragged wounded men, many of the same ones who abused him and even some who were the enemy, and lowered them off the cliff to medics waiting below. Despite intense fatigue and bloodied hands, he refused to stop until all the wounded he could save were off the ridge. When asked about his experience and how he could save so many, his response was simply, "I just kept telling myself to save one more—just one more!"

My favorite line from the movie was when he was being told to just quit and leave training camp before the war began, and he responded, "While everyone is busy taking lives, I'm going to be saving lives." No one ever questioned Desmond Doss after that. He was an all-in kind of guy.

Running Toward the Fight

Desmond Doss reminds me of the story we all know from 1 Samuel 17 where David the shepherd boy, in one event, transitions into David the warrior by slaying Goliath. David believed in God and his nation Israel, and he was not going to stand by and have a heathen Philistine shout down curses on the army of the Lord. 1 Samuel 17:48 says,

"When the Philistine arose and came and drew near to meet David, David ran quickly toward the battle line to meet the Philistine" (ESV).

David became a warrior that day, with no backing down and no excuses, but instead he ran toward the fight, toward the nine-foot-nine giant, and killed him with a slingshot and a stone.

Now, what about you? You may be thinking, *Well, I am no Desmond Doss, and I am not King David.* Again, it was intentional for me to focus on two unlikely heroes. Desmond went into WWII without a weapon and don't think of David as a king. He had just come from the fields as a young shepherd boy. Both were mocked and made fun of; both definitely shook their fists in the face of adversity and refused to back down until the job was done despite the obvious disadvantages they brought with them to the fight.

Now I get it. Sometimes the task is a little more unclear, and the course of action needed is rather confusing. So what then? How should we then respond? Have you ever been in a situation where you are absolutely and completely unsure of what to do next? Or have you ever felt so out of control where the very next step you should take is not visible and so frozen with fear you remain stuck feeling trapped and powerless? I mean, your heart is in it. You just don't know what to do.

Our Eyes Are on You

King Jehoshaphat, one of the kings of Judah, was facing this very situation, and it is worth sharing. Here is the scene: enemy nations were converging against him to destroy Judah. All his people knew of the pending doom, and they began to panic, but listen to his response in 2 Chronicles 20:3-4, "Then Jehoshaphat was afraid and set his face to seek the Lord ... and Judah assembled to seek help from the Lord" (ESV).

As Jehoshaphat prayed before the whole nation of Judah, he concludes with these words, "We are powerless against this great horde that is coming against us. We do not know what to do but our eyes are on you" (vs. 12 ESV).

Wait, here is the king who is supposed to have all the answers, the one who is supposed to have a game plan, the one who should lead them to victory in battle. And what is his response? After his initial human response of fear, he immediately goes to the Lord in prayer and leads his entire country to do the same. Wow! What a scene! All eyes are on him now, and the people can begin to sense that their demise as a nation is very possible, if not imminent. From his military leaders all the way down to the little children, they are leaning in, waiting for an encouraging word, a game plan, and a battle strategy from their king, and he finally concludes three things:

1. We are powerless,
2. We are unsure of what to do next, *but*
3. Our eyes are on you, God!

What incredible leadership! He knew that between the odds he was facing and his military limitations, his best move was to acknowledge his present situation and fix his eyes on The One far more powerful and capable than all the nations of the world. In essence, he prays to God that all of Judah, himself included, is waiting, watching, and listening to receive their orders from Him. He took the attention and focus off himself and directed an entire nation to be looking past him to see and seek God's face!

Let's linger here for a moment and soak in this lesson that King Jehoshaphat offers to us. Was he all in? You better believe it! This was his kingdom, but he knew who the true King was, and he was humble enough to acknowledge it before all his people and the true King of Kings! See how God responds.

Our All-In King

An answer came to Judah as the Lord answered through Jahaziel, a Levite, by saying, "Do not be afraid and do not be dismayed at this great horde, for the battle is not yours but God's. You will not need to fight in this battle. Stand firm, hold your position, and see the salvation of the Lord on your behalf" (2 Chronicles 20:15b, 17 ESV).

So wait, as a king who was all in, God tells him to stop the commotion, stop trying to fix it, and just watch. Yes, there it is once again where Scripture is telling us to stand still. How much extra effort, worry, and anxiety do we exert when we should be waiting and resting on the King to come through for us?

The result was that the Lord set an ambush and had three nations collide against one another with this recorded outcome, "When Judah came to the watchtower of the wilderness, they looked toward the horde, and behold, there were dead bodies lying on the ground; none had escaped" (2 Chronicles 20:24 ESV). Not one sword of Judah had to be unsheathed. The Lord did their fighting for them.

King Jehoshaphat modeled for us that to truly be all in actually looks like full and complete surrender to the true King of Kings as we follow His commands and orders.

So as we have already established, you are made in the image of our Great King. You are designed and created to act like Him as you look to Him. David ran quickly toward the challenge. Desmond Doss dragged one man after another to safety. Such are the lives of those who understand their identity, have a cause greater than themselves, and are fighting for a purpose in the strength of the Lord. As the ultimate example, Christ took the blade of death and, instead of deflecting the blow, grabbed it and pulled it in, embracing its pierce on behalf of you and me.

Courage Challenge

In your specific area of influence, what do you believe are the top one or two greatest needs for you to step up and exercise masculine courage? It is easy to identify those areas outside of our areas of influence. The need and void are all around us but make it personal to you! Use the following questions to guide your thoughts and then action steps:

1. What typically is your first response when faced with overwhelming odds? Is your first response "I got this" as you set about to work harder to try to figure it out, or is it to fight from your knees as you seek God's face for the next right move to take? Describe your response.

2. Share a time when you desperately wanted to stand in the gap for another person or a cause, but either because of personal fear or circumstances out of your control, this was either not possible or you just didn't have the courage to do it. (Identify the need.)

3. Where have you seen noble action taking place where someone has courageously stood in the gap for another or to right the wrong? As you observed, what conversation did you have with yourself at that time? Were you wishing that you were the one stepping to the front lines and winning the day?

4. In your area of influence, what do you believe is the greatest area of need that currently is not being addressed? Who else can stand in the gap with you? What will happen if nothing is done? (Don't assume someone else will just fill in for you.)

5. Where will you stand in the gap with courage and conviction? Identify the area of need where you will step in. Accept the challenge today!

6. Share the need where you will be stepping in with another person and ask them to follow up and ask you how it went.

Knowing accountability will be extended will be helpful to keep you from backing out and your courage from going underground.

7. How would you characterize your dependency upon God? Keep in mind that despite how we might feel for the moment, we are always needy, incompetent, inadequate, or inept in comparison to the God we serve. This could cause us to be desperately dependent on God. Jesus said, "apart from me you can do nothing" (John 15:5 ESV).

CHAPTER TEN

MY LIFE FOR YOURS

If anyone would come after me, let him deny himself
and take up the cross and follow Me.
—JESUS, MATTHEW 16:24 (ESV)

The ultimate test of man's conscience may be his
willingness to sacrifice something today for future
generations whose words of thanks will not be heard.
—GAYLORD NELSON[84]

Toward the Chaos

I will never forget watching the events of 9/11 unfold on the television screen on September 11, 2001. As the Twin Towers were burning, firefighter after firefighter ran into the chaos, the burning building, as people were doing everything they could to get out. I can recall how they ran, literally ran, toward the burning building. It was instinctive; it was part of their training. It was their mission at all costs and by all means. On that horrific day, 343 brave and courageous firefighters, while attempting to save the lives of others, sacrificed their very own lives in this noble and valiant last mission.

Many of us would quickly say that we would never sign up for such a job. Of course we can admire, respect, and honor such men from a distance, but seriously? Who would actually sign up to do such work where we could be called upon in a moment's notice to be willing and ready to surrender our very lives?

Job Description from Jesus

As someone who hires about ten to fifteen people each year, I spend a great deal of time creating job descriptions in hopes of finding the ideal candidate for each job opening. Each year, I review well over a hundred résumés from people who have responded to these two to three page-long job descriptions. Unlike such lengthy job descriptions, Jesus simply gives us three expectations He has for us that will mark us as one of His people: deny, carry, and follow.

First of all, it is important to know that the passage noted previously comes right on the heels of Jesus for the first time revealing to his disciples that he must suffer and die. Once revealed, Peter, in a style all his own, jumps in and rebukes Jesus by telling him this will never happen! In turn, Jesus firmly and soundly rebukes Peter for being used by Satan to hinder the very reason He came to earth.

But we already know this, right? After all, this was God's mission for Jesus. Yes, it was, and then it became our mission! Once Jesus reveals God's plan for Him, Jesus then reveals His plan for our lives. In Matthew 16:24, He gives us our job description when He tells us to deny self, take up our cross, and follow Him! Deny, carry, and follow. Let's look at each of these.

Deny Self

To deny self is to intentionally lose or die to yourself for the sake of the King and His kingdom's good and its gain. It is an utter rejection of self-will and self-sufficiency as well as a recognition of our complete and utter spiritual destitution. When we realize how poor we are, we can begin to recognize and know the riches of Christ! When we recognize our sinfulness, we can truly experience and appreciate God's grace. It is not the proud that Jesus justified but the brokenhearted and humble. It is the broken and contrite heart that God loves and will never despise (Psalm 51:17).

Carry Our Cross

The crucifixion is a shocking metaphor for discipleship. This is the ultimate form of denying one's will to embrace God's will regardless of the cost. It is the willingness to endure shame, embarrassment, reproach, rejection, persecution, and even martyrdom for His sake. To Jesus's listeners, this was a vivid and shocking picture of how downright serious Jesus was. To them, a man who took up his cross began His death march carrying the very beam on which He would hang. Not all the apostles were martyred, but all were ready and willing to do so.

This is why Peter writes to his fellow believers,

> Do not be surprised at the fiery trial when it comes upon you to test you, as though something strange were happening to you. But rejoice insofar as you share Christ's sufferings, that you may also rejoice and be glad when his glory is revealed. If you are insulted for the name of Christ, you are blessed, because the Spirit of glory and of God rests upon you. (1 Peter 4:12–14 ESV)

Some might desire a no-cost discipleship, but Jesus makes no such offer. To carry our cross is to do whatever God asks us to do, to pursue it with our whole heart, and to fully surrender.

Follow Me

Only after a person has denied himself and taken up his cross is he then prepared to follow Jesus! To accomplish these first two shows obedient submission and a heart prepared to walk in the same manner Jesus did (1 John 2:6). Jesus declared that "(He) who does the will of My Father who is in heaven" (Matthew 7:21 ESV) and he who continues in "my word, you are truly my disciples" (John 8:31 ESV). I'm sure you are getting the picture! Participation is not optional. Full and total investment is required!

Flipping the Script

On one level, this sounds rather simple, but we know this is actually very difficult. If we stop for a moment and actually think about this "deny, carry, and follow" command, it is so counter to how we have been raised all our lives. If honest, the script we have been writing and has been written for us by many around us, primarily our parents, is that life is all about me. We say, "It is all about my script. Others are only important to me and can only enter my story if and only if it will make my script better. And I want it to be better. I want my script to be read with great significance, incredible pleasures, unspeakable joys, inner and external peace, and happiness and contentment, which can come through applause, accolades, accommodations, and accomplishments. Should my script resemble this, then I may find satisfaction in life and in the end feel good about my life story. After all, isn't it really about me?"

A Snowflake Generation

As I write, football season is just around the corner. Last week I watched a father wait each morning for his son to come out of the locker room so he could hand him a Gatorade to drink and then carry his bag to the field. Mind you, this is a high school football player. Then after the practice was over, the father met his son as he came off the field, had another Gatorade for him, helped him out of his shoulder pads, and then carried these shoulder pads to the locker room for the young man.

Needless to say, our coaches had a word with this dad about how he was emasculating and crippling the young man to take responsibility and ownership and to handle a little bit of hardship.

Unfortunately, as our culture grows softer and softer, pursue the comforts of life, and strive for the most while giving the least, we find that our script begins to be written slightly different than what we have been told our whole life. We were made to believe life is about others pleasing and bowing to us; we are faced with hard life reality and unexpectant consequences that greets us with feelings of surprise, despair, depression, hopelessness, impatience, worry, anxiety, apathy, blame, anger, disappointment, disillusionment, discouragement, and a loss of joy.

Instead of Jesus's model of deny self, we have altered the narrative by saying "deny self nothing," thinking this will bring us true happiness and contentment. Yet stop and ask yourself which is better in the long run. Think about Christmastime. Do you enjoy giving or getting more? Of course we all enjoy getting. Sadly, we are a disposable culture addicted to the emotional boost of buying something new. It is estimated that in the United States in 2019, over $240 billion was spent in advertising![85] What is the messaging that we are bombarded with on a daily basis? The advertising industry is seeking to write on our script that our life is not complete and we will not be satisfied until we have whatever they are pushing toward us. One does not have to purchase too many things to know that dissatisfaction sets in very quickly. The 1965 Rolling Stones song "I Can't Get No Satisfaction" rings ever true sixty years later, and it will for the rest of our lives if our significance and value are wrapped up in what we have and what we receive.

But have you ever watched a youngster who has either made or bought something with their own money for a gift to another person?

They are so excited to give their gift. In Acts 20:35, Paul quotes Jesus when he says, "It is more blessed to give than to receive" (ESV).

More Does Not Equal Freedom

We believe that the more we have, the more we get, and the more freedom we can experience. However, the more one has, the more one has to worry about. I remember how much I wanted a ski boat. I thought this would be just an amazing way for our family to spend weekends skiing, wakeboarding, tubing, and fishing ... and we did! It was great until the moment I forgot to put in the drain plug when my son and I were out fishing one day, only to realize that the boat seemed lower to the water than normal. I lifted up the hatch to the housing for the twin jet engines, only to see that the compartment was filling up with water. I was finally able to get one engine working as we chugged back to the dock. However, the other engine had taken in water. This was not the last time I had to take the boat in to get it worked on. Needless to say, like most boat owners can testify to, the two best days of owning a boat are the day it was purchased and the day it was sold.

Self-Last

But let's get serious here. To deny oneself is far more than worldly possessions. Instead this literally is a call to put the lives of others before that of your own. John 15:13 says, "Greater love has no one than this, that he lay down his life for his friends" (NIV). Does that mean I have to be willing and ready to die for someone else? Maybe ... but it does not necessarily have to mean this.

Galatians 2:20 gives us a window into what this looks like when Paul says, "I have been crucified with Christ and I no longer live, but Christ lives in me. The life I now live in the body, I live by faith in the

Son of God, who loved me and gave himself for me" (NIV). In other words, when Christ died, our old man, the flesh, died with Him, and we no longer live a life that is all about us. Instead we willingly say "my life for yours." I am willing to inconvenience my life to convenience yours, however small or great that may be.

Willingly is an important word here. We see in John 10:17–18 where Jesus makes His intentions about His death explicitly clear as He says, "For this reason the Father loves me, because I lay down my life that I may take it up again. No one takes it from Me, but I lay it down of My own accord. I have authority to lay it down, and I have authority to take it up again" (ESV). Every step toward Calvary, every lash from the whip that tore flesh from His body, every hammer blow on the nails that drove into His hands, Jesus was saying, "This is for you because I love you!" Talk about flipping the script in epic proportions!

Romans 5:7–8 drives this idea home when it says, "For one will scarcely die for a righteous person—though perhaps for a good person one would dare even to die—but God shows His love for us in that while we were still sinners, Christ died for us" (ESV).

So as He did, we too must be putting the needs and lives of others before that of ourselves. Scripture makes this crystal clear, but what does this practically look like to deny ourselves, take up our cross or the burden the Lord has placed on our hearts, and follow or do what He would do? For one possessing true masculine courage like our Jesus, it looks like this: We must have the eyes to see the needs that are all around. The needs are there; the question is where we will have the eyes of Jesus to actually see them in a way that is deeply meaningful and significant and that causes something in your heart to stir.

In Matthew 9:36, we see Jesus going throughout the towns and villages where Matthew records, "When he saw the crowds, he had compassion on them, because they were harassed and helpless, like sheep without a shepherd" (ESV). Jesus didn't have to, but He chose to go to difficult places. As He went, he noticed the needs and was moved with compassion by what He saw. His heart hurt. What do you see? What are you noticing that makes your heart hurt? Are they the same things that burden and break the heart of Jesus?

Life-Giving Community

We are called to be men of action and to get off the sidelines and to initiate, knowing there will be a cost. You see, when Jesus would initiate with people and invite them into a relationship, they would receive love and communion with Him and the fellowship of other brothers and sisters along the way. Simultaneously, in the same life-giving community, it can be a place of great pain as our pride, brokenness, and fears are exposed. However, to be with a group of people as such, we discover that in all our inadequacies we are meant to be together, and we can even ask hard questions such as: Do I really matter or have any real value in this life? Does my life have any significance? Do you notice me? In true and meaningful community, the answers come back like the beautiful rays of sunshine that declare, "Yes, you are important! Yes, you matter and have great significance! Yes, I can trust you! Yes, I believe in you!"

The Conflict of Competition in Community

Yet, to get to this point, our view of others and our view of Jesus must change. As one who has competed all my life, I love competition. I have also grown to understand that competition in community is the death of community as it declares not just a winner but subsequently a loser. When we scamper up the ladder, it naturally means the competition is also pressed down. And who is the competition? Other people we are meant to be living in community with. However, the beauty of the matter is that for people who have been at the bottom of the ladder and found Jesus there, they understand that this is not an ascent to Jesus but rather the great descent, for in the going down, we find the One who has been beaten and crucified on our behalf. He does not approach us from a place of superiority sitting at the highest seat, but instead we see Him bending down with a towel, washing our feet before sitting down beside us over a meal where He refers to us as His friends. Wow…just pause and reflect on that for a moment.

It is one of the great paradoxes of the Christian faith that the way up is the way down. To understand this is freeing and liberating! We are accepted as we are, broken and needy sinners. So the heart of Jesus's message is not from a position of superiority but gentle humility and kindness. It is to say, "Love your enemies. Do good to those who criticize you and hate you. Pray for those who persecute and push you down and pursue reconciliation with all—whenever humanly possible!"

With these eyes and the tuning of our heart, our feet can now begin to move as we finally understand what it really means to deny ourselves. In the kingdom of God, there are no little people. This should remind us that no one is beneath us or not worth going to, and there is no task we can't handle as long as we go in the spirit, strength, and humility as Jesus modeled for us.

1. When you see the need, give, expecting nothing in return. Too often we are wanting equivalency both when someone has wronged us and even when we have done something nice for someone else. Instead freely give and simply bask in the joy of giving without thinking how your act of kindness will benefit you. We know from Philippians 2 that Jesus "emptied himself." In other words, He gave everything He had on His way to the cross, not necessarily asking you to literally give up your life but to disadvantage yourself to the benefit of another.

2. Forgive another when they have wronged you. I totally understand what I am asking. The pain of the wrongdoing hurts like mad, and this is the last thing on your mind. However, as Jesus hung on the cross, He was offering

forgiveness as life was eking from His body. Acknowledging the hurt is fine; withholding forgiveness is not.

3. Carry the burden of others. Since our first parents, God did not mean for us to live alone but are meant to do life with others. To hurt when someone else is hurting, to sit in deep pain and sadness, even without saying a word, can be a priceless act of love. Recently my oldest son, Josh, a director of high school youth ministries at his church, had the difficult task of comforting five sons who tragically lost their mother in a head-on car collision. However, his care extended beyond these boys but also to others in the youth group as parents relayed to me how he was helping their children process through this tragedy and grief. Such people at the intersection of big life moments can make the difference between a downward spiral of despair or of finding hope in the midst of deep anguish.

4. As you see others, assign value to them greater than what you have assigned to yourself. If you can make this adjustment in your mind, then you will not only be able to see the needs around you but will have the heart and compassion to be moved to love and care for them. A proud person cannot learn and grow because they don't believe someone of lesser value has anything to teach them. Be humble and learn and grow in the process. You may well be a blessing to others along the way.

5. Love even when the love is not reciprocated. You will be surprised how time has a way of working on someone's heart. Over the years, I have had some very mean things lobbed in my direction as a high school principal. In honesty, I have not wanted to love some folks back. After all, this is not in my nature, and it is way too easy to justify why I shouldn't. However, we have the cross of Jesus to look to and are called to a cruciform love where everything we say and do should shape, mold, and resemble what Christ did on the cross. Our cross-shaped lenses inform the love we are to have for all in our lives, even those who irritate and are irrational and unreasonable. The cross frees us from the bondage of sin and

self where we can freely love even when we are not loved or even hated in return.

If at any point while reading this chapter you said to yourself, "Wait, I thought this book was about masculine courage. What is all this stuff about loving, serving, forgiving, and carrying others' burdens?" Think about Jesus' defining moment. He could have flexed His masculine muscles in a moment and wiped out the Roman centurions. He could have established His kingdom on earth and set up the Jewish people to overthrow the Romans right then and there. While watching Mel Gibson's *The Passion*, I found myself getting caught up in the movie and wishing Jesus would just rise up and grab the whip from the soldier who, with his smug and arrogant-looking face, was ripping the flesh from the King of the Universe, and fiercely turn the whip on His attacker instead. Of course, that would have been easy. It would have seemed to have been the masculine thing to do, it would have been a great ending to the movie and I would have stood and applauded.

However, Jesus had scripted a far different ending. His ending of the script was that His masculine nature would not go underground but rather would be on full display where He would exhibit the greatest act of love, the highest degree of service in complete and utter surrender to His Father. In so doing, He gave the highest degree of value and worth to image-bearers like you and me who are created in the image of His Father. This act by our Lord and Savior Jesus Christ was undeniably the greatest masculine act ever accomplished, and now we are called to image the one who modeled how we are to act as men.

Courage Challenge

Of the five ways one can die to self or be able to say "my life for yours," do the following:

1. Journal at least one way in which someone has done this for you. After reflecting and writing, if possible, take a moment and thank them. A personal face-to-face would be best. If this is not possible, then a phone call or even an email or text, but reach out! It will be an encouragement to them. Stop – don't let this moment pass you by.

2. Journal at least one way in which you have done this for another person and how you were blessed through the process.

3. Write a plan of how you will initiate at least one of the five areas noted on how one can deny self. Share the plan with a close friend and then go and carry out that plan. The plan has to move from a good idea to a plan set into motion where you engage with other people. While you will be a blessing, I can promise you that in the action you take, you too will be personally blessed.

CHAPTER ELEVEN

DO NOT WASTE YOUR WEAKNESSES

But he said to me, "My grace is sufficient for you, for my power is made perfect in weakness." Therefore I will boast all the more gladly of my weaknesses, so that the power of Christ may rest upon me. For the sake of Christ, then, I am content with weaknesses ... For when I am weak, then I am strong.
—2 CORINTHIANS 12:9–10 (ESV)

Deny your weakness, and you will never realize God's strength in you.[86]
—JONI EARECKSON TADA

Strength Attraction

I find it interesting that comic heroes that have been around for nearly a century are not only still relevant but are the rage with both teen and adult men. Superman first came on the scene in 1938 and Batman in 1939, and from there, superheroes were added over time, as we saw Captain America (1941), the Incredible Hulk (1962), Spider-Man (1962), Captain Marvel (1967), and then an explosion of new superheroes with the Marvel movies today. *Avengers: Endgame* brought in $2.1 billion worldwide, making it the highest-grossing

Marvel film of all time.[87] The Marvel films have only been in production since 2007, and in that time (2007–2019), Marvel Studios has produced and released twenty-three films. It is the highest-grossing film franchise of all time, having grossed over $22.5 billion at the global box office.[88]

I would find it shocking to find a man who has not seen at least one superhero movie, let alone been one of those guys who stood in line for an opening night premiere showing of an Avengers movie, hoping to be one of the first in the door to see the newest superhero flick. However, this idea of superheroes or almost superhuman strength and feats is not new to this world. One only has to look at Scripture and see some true stories of amazing recordings of what real men have done in the past. Check out some of these true recordings of Scripture.

Real Superhumans

- Eleazar was considered one of David's top three guys from his platoon of mighty men. He was a ferocious warrior who earned a reputation as a killing machine. His claim to fame is that during a battle with the Philistines, he annihilated so many of the enemy that by the end of the day he literally couldn't let go of his sword. He had been gripping his sword so tightly that his fingers had to be pried from the sword's handle. As one of the three mighty men, he was with David when they taunted the Philistines gathered for battle. Then the men of Israel retreated, but he stood his ground and struck down the Philistines until his hand grew tired and froze to the sword. The Lord brought about a great victory that day. The troops returned to Eleazar but only to strip the dead (2 Samuel 23:9–10 NIV). Based on this passage, it appears as though he was a one-man wrecking machine as Israel left and then came back once all the killing by Eleazar was done. What a scene that must have been!

- Benaiah, son of Jehoiada, a valiant fighter from Kabzeel, performed great exploits. He struck down two of Moab's best men. He also went down into a pit on a snowy day and killed a lion. And he struck down a huge Egyptian. Although the Egyptian had a spear in his hand, Benaiah went against him with a club. He snatched the spear from the Egyptian's hand and killed him with his own spear (2 Samuel 23:20–21 NIV). By the way, while all these feats are incredible, who jumps into a pit with slippery snow to kill a lion?

- Josheb-basshebeth, a Tahchemonite, was chief of the three. He wielded his spear against eight hundred, whom he killed at one time (2 Samuel 23:8 ESV). This might have been one of the scariest battle scenes ever as one man stood his ground and killed eight hundred people in one day, and this is hand-to-hand combat as he battled with only a spear. Such a feat earned him the leader or captain of David's mighty men, which seems like a pretty good choice to me.

- What the Hulk is to the Avengers, Samson is to the mighty men of the Bible. Most of Samson's problems had to do with his pursuit of a woman and usually a Philistine (the enemy) woman. In retaliation to the destruction that Samson caused in Philistia, the Philistines burned his wife and father-in-law to death. This is where things went from bad to worse for the Philistines. Judges 15:15–16 says, "And he found a fresh jawbone of a donkey, and put out his hand and took it, and with it he struck 1,000 men. And Samson said, 'With the jawbone of a donkey, heaps upon heaps, with the jawbone of a donkey have I struck down a thousand men'" (ESV). What a scene! To grab on to just how incredible this is, think about it this way: With only a jawbone of a donkey (a bone), he single-handedly killed a thousand men. I wonder when after 250 or 500 men had been killed, why did men hang around and not just call it a day and leave … like run? Even with an average kill time of one minute, it would still take him sixteen hours to kill a thousand people. Obviously this was done in the strength of the Lord as such endurance and survival from such an attempt has never nor ever could be replicated again.

A Call to Strength

So whether in today's fantasy culture through movies like the Marvel series or some of these great feats we see accomplished in Scripture, as men we are attracted to strength, we too desire to be strong, we wish to flex our muscles and to come through for others, and we usually wish we had more than we do. We go to the gym to increase our physique, we read and learn to strengthen our mental capacities, and we exercise authority over the places we have been entrusted to lead. This is not only natural but actually a mandate from God, who in the cultural mandate says to Adam to "take control and have dominion." God put Adam in charge. Adam was to lead and exhibit the strength and courage God had given him in his created and designed being. We see in Ephesians 6:10 where Paul is talking about the armor of God, and he concludes with, "Finally, be strong in the Lord and in the strength of his might" (ESV).

Most organizations at one time or another will often have their employees take some kind of personality tests to figure out how one can best serve their organization and work alongside their fellow teammates or co-workers. I have taken the Myers-Briggs several times, I have twice taken the Clifton Strengths Test, and of course a co-worker coerced me into taking the Enneagram Test. Of the Clifton Strengths Test, where one is given their top five, or most dominant, strengths from the thirty-four themes, my results came back as Belief, Achiever, Arranger, Activator, and Connectedness. In summary, I have core values that are enduring, and I live by (Belief). I have an internal fire and a drive to accomplish much every single day (Achiever). I am a conductor working with all the variables to help create the most productive configuration in a complex problem (Arranger). I am action-oriented. I can make decisions and am eager to get started (Activator), and I feel the need to work collaboratively and build bridges for and with others (Connectedness). The first time I took the test, instead of Connectedness, the results came back as Relator being one of my top five strengths.

Naturally I can learn a great deal about myself by studying these results. And as you can imagine, if you know anything about the Enneagram Test, I am an eight. Positive words for an eight are self-confident, strong, assertive, protective, decisive, straight-talking, and resourceful. By now, you likely are growing rather tired hearing about me, and up to this point, it appears as though I have it all together and think pretty highly of myself. In fact, you might be thinking, *Why the earth is he writing any of this in a chapter entitled "Do Not Waste Your Weaknesses"?* Here is the reality: for every strength, there is a shadow side that we either are told to minimize, reduce, hide, ignore, or even deny that such a weakness exists.

Yet based on the words I have shared about the eight Enneagram status, you could quickly look up on the internet that the shadow side of such a person is also that they can be egocentric and domineering, feel as though they must control their environment, or are confrontational and sometimes intimidating. In fact, an eight can have temper problems and struggle to allow themselves to be vulnerable. Whoa! A little too much information, right?!

Whether all these strengths and weaknesses listed are actually accurate about me or you (fellow eights), the reality is this: every single one of us has some strengths that we bring to our areas of influence, but despite what we either have been told, are made to think, or have convinced ourselves of, we all have weaknesses. And instead of living in denial or seeking to hide them, we must discover, uncover, reveal, confront, and admit that these exist and figure out how we can live fully out of these weaknesses. Why is this important?

As you will soon see, weakness is not only a major theme in the

Bible but is at the very heart of the gospel. For us to live as masculine, courageous men, it is to not just for us to live robust and vigorous lives from our strengths but to be vulnerable and transparent from a place of weaknesses and brokenness, for in such places, that's where Christ meets us.

Heroes of Weakness

Let step back into the Bible and catch a glimpse of our Bible superheroes again. I have listed ten men who were top of the list. These guys are the first man to live, first king of Israel, first missionary in history, humblest man, strongest man, man after God's own heart, wisest man, only man to walk on water, actually physically wrestled with God, and father of the faith. These guys are best of the best. If there is a Navy Seal Team Six equivalent, these guys are on the team! It is hard to find another top ten of the greatest men of the Bible. Let's take a closer look at them:

- Adam was the first man. He was also a blame shifter who caved to peer pressure and messed up the world for all humanity (Genesis 3:12).
- Abraham was the forefather of the faith, but twice let other men walk off with his wife because he was a coward and afraid or, better said, lacked faith that God would protect him (Genesis 12 and 20).
- Jacob was a man who all-out wrestled with God but was a pathological liar (Genesis 25, 27, 30).
- Moses was the humblest man on earth (Numbers 12:13) and yet had an anger problem and was a murderer (Exodus 2, 32:19; Numbers 20:11).
- Saul, the first king of Israel, had manic outbursts of anger and episodes of deep depression and even paranoia (1 Samuel 16, 18–19).

- Samson was the strongest man in the world, yet lust was his downfall (Judges 16:20–21).
- David, the friend of God/man after God's own heart, concealed his adultery by murdering Bathsheba's husband (2 Samuel 11).
- Solomon, the wisest man in the world, was likely the world's worst sex addict with a thousand wives/concubines (1 Kings 11).
- Jonah, the first recorded missionary, was prejudiced and a racist (Jonah 1).
- Peter walked on water and was an apostle of Jesus who performed miracles. He was a bold preacher, yet he was impulsive, denied Jesus publicly, and lacked faith (Matthew 14:22–33; Luke 22:59-62).

Can you now begin to relate to these superheroes? Suddenly the Bible stories are brought to our level! Some of the very greatest men of the Bible that God chose to use also struggled with major serious issues. We are talking about racism, adultery, sex addiction, womanizer, murder, anger, lying, depression, weak in faith, and cowardice, and the list goes on. But we could go through many of Jesus's disciples, and we would have another list of areas with which they too struggled.

Here is the point: God uses and works through the weak and struggling sinner. If you think that God can't use you because of areas of struggle in your life, remind yourself of these superheroes of the Bible and how God used them in mighty, powerful ways.

Weakness Is Strength

The apostle Paul got it. He struggled with a weakness, and while he earnestly prayed the Lord would take it from him, the response from the Lord instead was, "My grace is sufficient for you, for my power is made perfect in weakness" (2 Corinthians 12:9 ESV). So the answer that Paul in essence is getting is that your weakness, your struggle, that thorn in your side, is not going anywhere. It is there to stay. However, God's also saying, so am I, and I am going to use you in ways you don't even begin to understand. It will be through this weakness, in spite of it, I am going to do amazing things!

Paul concludes, "Therefore I will boast all the more gladly of my weaknesses, so that the power of Christ may rest upon me. For the sake of Christ, then, I am content with weaknesses ... For when I am weak, then I am strong" (2 Corinthians 12:9–10 ESV). What is Paul saying here? He is saying that "weakness is strength!"

Dan Allender, author of *Leading with a Limp*, put it this way, "He calls us to brokenness, not performance; to relationships, not commotion; to grace, not success."[89] Paul's summary of his life is summed up in three words, "chief of sinners." Paul is not bragging of his sin, he is not showing false humility, and he is not minimizing his sin but instead has come to an honest assessment of his position before a Holy God.

In 1 Timothy 1:15–16 (NIV), Paul says,

> Here is a trustworthy saying that deserves full acceptance: Christ Jesus came into the world to save sinners—of whom I am the worst. But for that very reason I was shown mercy so that in me, the worst of sinners, Christ Jesus might display his unlimited patience as an example for those who would believe on Him and receive eternal life.

Don't miss what Paul is saying here. Paul has dropped all pretense. Paul knows he is a mess and that before a righteous God, his very best is filthy rags, so let's just be honest and transparent about the whole matter.

Dan Allender says, "The leader who fails to face (their) darkness must live with fear and hypocrisy. The result will be defensiveness that places saving face and controlling others as higher goods than blessing others and doing good work."[90]

This is a game-changer. When things don't go right, there is no need to exercise the art of blame shifting but to instead show extreme ownership that the fault and blame lie within. Instead of receiving this as a shame or possible guilt and being riddled with fear, find great comfort in the reality and opportunity to just be broken before others.

Brokenness Is a Gift

Unless you have found yourself in a place of brokenness, this idea sounds foreign … unless it becomes the only option available to you. We don't necessarily go looking for brokenness; instead it finds us. As I spoke of in chapter 4, brokenness is not a choice but rather a gift. We find ourselves in unusual territory where no tracks have yet been laid and there's no go-to routine to follow. Instead we head into a time and place of the unknown that is unnerving, but there, we find God in a new and revealing way. As you stop running and simply fall into His embrace with utter surrender, God now has our undivided attention. We may be fatigued, worn, wounded, and hurting, and yet we are in the very best place we could be, just like Peter as he stepped out of the boat. Despite the winds and the waves that, for a moment, drew His attention away from Jesus, in reality he was closest to Jesus at that moment. If that had been you or me and we were to find ourselves out on the open water and starting to sink, to be near Jesus is a good place to be, actually the very best place to be!

It's Not About Me Anymore

Paul says, "I have been crucified with Christ. It is no longer I who live, but Christ who lives in me. And the life I now live in the flesh I live by faith in the Son of God, who loved me and gave himself for me" (Galatians 2:20 ESV). Here, Paul is not talking about his weakness, being broken but rather having died, putting to death the old man and now recalling to mind that Christ lives inside of him (us). As stated earlier, Paul uses the phrase "in Him" over 160 times in his writings. In Ephesians 1:1–14, we see at least six times Paul says, "In Him … we have been chosen, in Him we are redeemed and forgiven, in Him we are united to Him, in Him we get an inheritance, in Him we believe the Truth, in Him we have been sealed by the Holy Spirit already!" (NIV).

What is he driving at? This is not our life. We have been bought with a price through the blood of Jesus Christ. It was a hero dying for villains, victory through death, life arising from death, the dark giving way to the dawn. With Christ in us, then He will work through us. As a result of our weaknesses, others can see, watch, marvel, and then say, "There is no way that person did that. Obviously God showed up and helped him through and then created a way where there was no way." That's why we can sing of the Waymaker!

The ceiling and limits have been removed. We can dream big knowing that He is a God who knows no limits and has no bounds and our weaknesses, regardless of how big or small, will never limit, restrict, or hold Him back from accomplishing that which He wills. The sooner we realize and embrace this, the more readily we can be used as an instrument for His kingdom advancement.

Courage Challenge

1. Discover your weaknesses:
   a. Personality Test(s): If you have taken any personality test in the past, go back and look not just at the strengths but also the weaknesses or shadow side of the strengths assigned to you.
   b. Truth-Teller: If you have never taken a personality test before, ask the three people who know you the best what the weaknesses are that they see in your life. Bottom line, you need a truth-teller in your life who can shoot straight and tell it to you like it is. Everyone one of us has blind

spots in our lives, and these obviously need to be revealed to us because we are blind to them.

    c. Personal Reflection and Assessment: Identify patterns of when and where the weakness(es) are manifested.

2. Share your weaknesses with others. There is little that will bring a group of people, large or small, together than for there to be open, honest, transparent, and vulnerable conversations, especially if it leads to confession and repentance. I often will tell our teachers that there are few sets of words that can turn a classroom around completely after you have made a mistake and really messed up than to use any of these three phrases as your starting point, "I was wrong," "I am sorry, " or "Please forgive me." Remember that your weakness can be your strength if you acknowledge it, confess it if need be, and keep moving forward, knowing that God loves to work through weak, broken, confessing, and repenting men.

3. Finally make it your prayer to the Lord to use you as a result of these weaknesses. God is a big God. Don't limit Him in your prayers. (There are times that I think, *Who is going to want to read what I have to say? Who am I kidding, working to write another book?* Well, despite this insecurity on my part, something must have gone right if you have read to chapter 10. Haha!) If God has given you a vision like Moses to free His people, don't let a speech impediment stand in your way. Take your situation and your weakness. You can count on God meeting you right there because with Christ "in you," He is where you are and will guide you to where you are to be doing what He desires for you to do!

Chapter Twelve

COURAGE FUEL

And when they found him, they exclaimed: "Everyone is looking for you!" Jesus replied, "Let us go somewhere else … "
—Mark 1:37b–38a (NIV)

Quietude … is as a palace of cedar to the wise, for along its hallowed courts the King in His beauty deigns to walk.
—Charles H. Spurgeon[91]

Everyone Is Looking for You

Have you ever found yourself in a similar situation to the one Jesus's disciples find him in? Have you ever felt as though there simply is not enough of you to go around to meet the needs you feel you must meet or that others have imposed upon you? If you are like most men, at some point in time, you have experienced this press that demands your time and attention, but not just some of it—all of it!

Even if you gave everything you had, it still seems as though this would simply not be enough to make it happen. After all, isn't that our deal as guys? We are supposed to come through and show that we have what it takes to get the job done, to meet the needs, to make the boss happy, to make ends meet, and to get that promotion that would provide additional income to rise up and save the day?! We have been conditioned to believe that our worth and value is in our ability to come through for others and to perform, perform, and perform, at least if we want to be relevant and stay current … and of course that target is changing constantly.

Of course, we know that Jesus can easily do this, but what is going on that would cause the disciples to be in a panic as they search for him? The preceding verses tell us that Jesus had been making it happen for the townspeople, as in Mark 1:32–34 he records, "The whole town gathered at the door and Jesus healed many who had various diseases. He also drove out many demons …" (NIV).

Get the picture? The whole town was pressing in on him to perform spectacular miracles! Sit on these words here for a moment. The whole town was gathered. This is not a doctor's visit, where appointments are set up and one at a time people are coming to meet Jesus. This is an event where the entire town is pressing in at the door of the house where Jesus was. What a scene! Jesus is almost pinned down at the house as they meet Him at the door and stand there late into the evening to either receive or watch Him do spectacular miracles.

Can you imagine the affirmation, celebration, and the cheering and excitement that was surrounding this impromptu healing event? The disciples were loving it that their guy, the hero, was coming through, meeting all the needs of the people in the town doing these amazing healing acts and miracles.

As a guy, I get it. It is fun to come through for others and see great progress being made, with people happy and satisfied. There is something wholesome, good, and beautiful in all this.

The Thrill and Delusion of Coming Through

So what about you? Go to that time and place when you were the hero, people were patting you on the back, your stock was up, and people just couldn't get enough of you. You were recognized, affirmed, validated, and celebrated, and it seemed as though everyone wanted to be your friend and be in on the parade in your honor.

But what had you done that made people respond in such a way? A bit of my story ... For me, I started out as a teacher and soccer coach. In my first year coaching varsity high school soccer, fresh right out of college, we won the school's first ever state championship in soccer. After two years of teaching, I was asked to be the junior high principal at twenty-four years of age, and by twenty-nine, I had my doctorate degree and was the president (headmaster) of a well-established K-12 private school. It doesn't take long, particularly when affirmed at a rather young age, to begin to find one's identity wrapped up in one's successes as affirmation and validation are thrown your direction.

Don't get me wrong here. There is nothing wrong with working hard and pursuing excellence and for others to notice, recognize, and appreciate what you have done. So what is the problem? The problem is twofold: motive and time. Let me speak to both. If my motive for doing what I do is wrapped up in what I will get as a result of my hard work and all that goodness that I hope to be able to produce, there develops a shadow side to it all, as it will lead to complete slavery and bondage to the applause and recognition of others. This is not only the wrong motivation, it is unsustainable.

I have worked in four school settings over twenty-seven years. What I have noticed is that each time I started a new job, there was an outpouring of appreciation for the enthusiasm and energy I brought to my work. However, after being able to sustain that over a period of time, that no longer was the new and exciting, but the expected and the less affirmed as the new norm becomes established. So what is one to do that loves to not just come through for others but to be affirmed and validated for their work but to do more, work harder, and be more creative and more innovative? Hopefully in time, it will garner the attention so longed for and desired.

Such a perspective is the result of misaligned motives. The life of a man of masculine courage is to, out of humble submission and obedience to the Great King, do everything to bring the Lord honor and glory, for it is only through Him that anything good is remotely possible. In other words, the spotlight should never be on us, but we should always be glory-deflectors when things go well. Even then this is a challenge as we can exercise false humility as we minimize the effort it took to accomplish the task, all the while basking in the praise being heaped on us.

The second problem with the striving and driving for success mentality for the external feedback and the praise of men is that there is not enough time to always be coming through for others without compromising and cutting corners in places that matter most and where the stakes are the absolutely highest. I'm talking about deep meaningful relationships, which often means those waiting at home for us. The old adage that dads can be "heroes at work and zeroes at home" is due to the fact that real life actually happens when we walk through the door to greet our wife or kids at the end of eight-plus hours of saving the universe at work. We walk through the door, and the Superman cape just seems to fall off as reality kicks in because bills have to be paid, lawns need to be mowed, things need to get fixed, kids have homework, the house and cars need maintenance, and family meals and conversations must take time … not to mention that the family is waiting for Dad to lead them spiritually.

This is not just about some guys out there who need to pull it together and just be better. Frankly, this hits close to home for many guys today, especially the one writing the words you are now reading, as much of this is my story. It pains me to say this and write these words, but let's go behind the curtain for a moment. I have an absolutely incredible wife and three amazing sons! I couldn't have asked for anything more in life! Period! Yet over the years I could have and should have prioritized them more than I did. Even as I write these words, my head tells my heart to defend why you have worked so hard and done what you have done, and yet my heart knows that to do so would be the work of a traitor. My heart knows all too well that the praise and approval of others has held a place in my heart that is not only unhealthy but has prioritized and set up systems and patterns aimed at striving and driving for more of the same. The more outcome task-oriented I became over time, the more slight setbacks would bother me.

For example, as a soccer coach, I have been to the state championship match ten times out of twenty-six years of coaching varsity soccer. Some coaches may go a career and not get to the title game. Yet the Lord has graciously allowed me to be the coach that won five times out of those ten title opportunities. Most would think this is great, but if honest, I have been frustrated with myself that I didn't do this or that to have put our teams in a position to perform better. Yes, reflection, evaluation, and adjustments to be able to perform better are all good and fine things, even necessary.

Yet let's remember that I am speaking of motive for what causes us to do what we do. None of this is easy stuff here because if I were simply talking about being hardworking and accomplishing certain tasks, that is easy to assess as plenty of people can evaluate whether we checked enough boxes and did what we said we were going to do. It is an entirely different matter to speak of motive because that is a matter that can really only be settled between a man and his God.

When I put my head on my pillow at night and in the quietness or sometimes the roaring of my own thoughts, it is just God and me. I have to come face-to-face with the realization that I can fool no one. I can try to fool the world and convince others through my actions that my motives are right, true, and pure, but at the end of the day, if I am not true and honest with myself and my holy, all-knowing, and all-seeing God, then I have deceived and misled everyone by my less than genuine actions and responses.

I'm slowly learning that setbacks, disruptions, and disappointments are not only part of normal life but are actually good! The Lord has used these times in my life to remind me of God's sovereignty over all of life, and that, for me, refinement work needs to happen, that He needs to get my attention and I need to refocus priorities and allow God to reset my agenda. For younger readers, please hear me well that the sooner one realizes this in life, the better off you will be. Maybe what follows will help to illustrate this.

Hitting the Wall

As an athlete (former) and a coach, I know all too well what happens when hard effort expends over a sustained period of time without adequate hydration and proper rest. Oftentimes we see it from athletes at the start of a season when the heat is turned up, the game is winding down, and suddenly a player goes down to the ground, grabbing his calves or hamstrings that are seizing up on him. The body is screaming out that they are being overworked and pushed too hard. The muscles are speaking to us, saying they were not taken care of like they should have been.

When an athlete's glycogen levels run low, the body begins to tap into fat reserves, and that is what they are, reserves. They are not there to sustain you for a long period of time, and if something is not done quickly, the body will shut down and no longer be able to perform. And I am not talking about its inability to perform at peak capacity, but instead the body's inability to perform at any capacity at all! I have not just witnessed this much too often with athletes but have experienced this in my own life, and it is a painful experience when that muscle is contracting and seems as though it just will not release but stay in the tightening position forever.

We can learn a great deal about life by learning how the body operates. In our striving and driving, at times we must practically tap into the reserves when working late in the office, taking work calls at home, sitting at home answering work emails, picking up an extra shift, or missing a child's game may be unavoidable. But to make this the norm for our life and what those around us should come to expect is not only unsustainable but puts life on a crash course where the ramifications are potentially irreversible.

Just in the last couple weeks, I have had several close friends whose marriages are in serious trouble. In the world's eyes, these are successful men who are making an impact in their place of employment. Success has found its way to their front door and has beckoned for them to follow into the deep waters of accomplishments, promotions, and plaudits. The money, attention, and accolades have blinded them from the necessary vision required to see that the warning lights on their dashboard have been flashing and they simply missed them, usually completely ignoring the warning signs.

I remember when one of my sons came home one day and said, "Dad, the engine light has been on for a while in my car. Is that something we should look into?"

"What?" I exclaimed. "What do you mean it has been on for a while? How long is a while because when the engine light comes on, that is not something to just have a hunch that everything likely is fine and just keep on driving?"

In the same way, when the important relationships in our life start to come undone and the stress, demands, pressures, fatigue, long hours, sleep deprivation, confrontation, and feelings of being worn out, overworked, burdened, strained, criticized, tested, confused, misunderstood, misconstrued, misrepresented, lonely, rejected, abandon, ignored, suffering, hated, or burdened hit eerily close to home, something must change. This is not something to ignore and just assume it will get better. It means to pull the car over, lift the hood, and do a serious check on the engine (see chapter 1 again) because if that stops working, nothing good is happening. In a similar way, what is the ripple effect or possibly the tsunami that could be initiated as a result of you checking out, faltering, or striking out?

Actually stop and think about this scenario. How will your actions define the life of those closest to you? One night I was having dinner with my oldest son, Josh, a twenty-one-year-old senior at Covenant College where he is a biblical studies/youth ministry major and plays on the men's soccer team. We were talking about the game they had just played where they had beat Berry College 2-0 and he had a goal and an assist and was leading all Division III colleges in the nation with assists at the time. (See what I did there, list my son's current soccer accolades.)

I recalled with him the time we were driving back from a youth soccer game on Lookout Mountain. That particular day he had scored four goals. As we were driving, he turned and looked at me and then asked, "Dad, do you love me more since I scored four goals?"

I immediately pulled the car over, put my hands on his shoulders, and said, "Josh, my love for you is not tied to your performance on the field. If you score hundreds of goals, I won't love you more, and if you never score another goal, I will not love you less."

Our actions are not our own but instead affect those around us far more than we think or wish to admit. Obviously I must have said something, possibly earlier on Saturday where he wondered if my love were conditional to his performance.

You are too valuable, you are needed too much, you have significance, and if you hear any different message, you are listening to the wrong people. The Great Deceiver wants you gone, out of the picture, disengaged, and put on the disabled list, unable to be called up for active duty! No! It is not time to resign or retire, but it is time to renew, refire, and reengage as one reinvigorated. However, when you hit the wall, you know too well that it does not give much and depending on how hard you hit that wall, it can leave a mark or even deep wounding. And yet reengage you must.

Water in the Desert

So let's go back to the story. After all, what was Jesus doing when the disciples finally found Him? At first glance, Jesus had in the wee hours of the morning slipped away when no one was watching. We get that, right? Sometimes we just need to step away from the fray to find space. We certainly don't second-guess Jesus for this decision (or any decision He made, just to go on record as saying that).

Jesus stepped away early in the morning for the specific purpose as Scripture says, to do the following, "And rising very early in the morning, while it was still dark, he departed and went to a desolate place, and there he prayed" (Mark 1:35 ESV). This idea was not a novel, one-time event with Jesus. This actually was a consistent pattern we see all through the gospels. Look at some of these examples:

- "And having sent away the crowds, he went up on the <u>mountain</u> to <u>pray</u> privately. And when evening came, he was there alone." (Matthew 14:23)
- "And very early in the morning when it was still quite dark, Jesus rose up, left the house, and went out to a lonely place, and there he prayed." (Mark 1:3)
- "But he retired into the wilderness and prayed." (Luke 5:16)
- "In those days he went out to the mountain to pray; and he spent the whole night in prayer with God." (Luke 6:12)

Notice that the getting away was not to unplug or to disengage, but instead He stepped away for deliberate refueling before reengaging. There was no cell phones, music, TV, multitasking, or people. No distraction! Notice how Jesus was focused and single-minded as He sought out seclusion and silence for exclusivity with His Father. Jesus's rhythm of life was intense ministry, and then He would withdraw to pray as He refueled to reengage priorities to resume another period of intense ministry. How often are we red-lining it as we come dangerously close to stalling out as we attempt to run on fumes anyway?

I know this may be a guy thing, but at times my fuel light will come on, and I want to see how far I can get that needle down and still be able to get to the gas station. In some ways, it is a little adventure, sick though it may be. It drives my wife nuts, so I will rarely do that when she is in the car. But isn't there some truth to this in how we live our lives. We see just how far down we can drop that red line and keep running on fumes. It is almost like some warped badge of courage.

"My red light came on, and I drove another thirty-six miles!"

"Oh really, when mine came on, I drove for forty-three miles and coasted into the closest gas station! That was close."

Well, if you have ever run out of gas on an interstate with no station nearby and no gas can, you have put yourself in a real predicament, one that likely could have been avoided, and now you feel like a real silly for making some of the decisions that got you into that position.

Looking back at the story of Jesus, some might read this and say, "Well, yeah, that is Jesus. Of course, He had a special connection to the Father, but He was part of the Trinity Himself."

Sure, this is true, but if this is Jesus's go-to response when He was nearing exhaustion, then should we not also follow suit? You might feel as though you have tried, but it seems that God is distant or silent. These are two natural responses when we don't hear from Him in the moment we want to hear from him. Sometimes we get a "yes" or "no", or other times it is simply a "not yet." Or we are to stay engaged in the conversation with no sense of the next step to take. If you have felt this way, then know that you stand in good company. Take a look at a few of the great men of the Bible who struggled in this very same way:

- Moses
  o "Why have you brought this trouble on your servant" (Numbers 11:11 NIV)?
  o "Is the arm of the Lord too short" (Numbers 11:23 NIV)?
- Habakkuk
  o "How long, O Lord, must I call for help, but you do not listen" (Habakkuk 1:2 NIV)?
  o "Why are you silent while the wicked swallow up those more righteous than themselves" (Habakkuk 1:13 NIV)?
- Job
  o "I cry out to you, O God, but you do not answer, I stand up, but you merely look at me" (Job 30:20–31 NIV).
- David
  o "O Lord, how long will you look on" (Psalm 35:17 NIV)?
  o "Hear me, O God, as I voice my complaint" (Psalms 64:1–2 NIV).
- Paul
  o "Three times I pleaded with you to take it (my thorn) away from me" (2 Corinthians 12:8–9 NIV).

Of all the things I could say on prayer, why would I list such open-ended and apparent unanswered pleas and cries for help? I do so because in most fights, there is a prolonged struggle when the outcome is uncertain. Quick fixes and easy answers are what we want but rarely get. Instead in a prolonged and sustained dialogue with our King, we at times find that our requests begin to align with His will. Our thoughts merge with His thoughts. If we stand to and stay in the fighting position long enough, we begin to sound like Samuel, who Eli told to "Speak, Lord, for your servant is listening" (1 Samuel 3:9 NIV). In our patient, humble submission to God's will, we begin to hear Him respond. It well may be that He was responding all along, but we were dialed into the wrong station. We had failed to tune into His voice, searching for His will, but were simply waiting and wishing for Him to fall in line with our will and our way.

God does not work that way and certainly is not bound to any time constraint. In 1 Samuel 3:18b, we see such an example shared by Eli to Samuel when Eli said, "He is the Lord; let Him do what is good in His eyes" (NIV).

Be encouraged. "The prayer of a righteous man is powerful and effective" (James 5:16 NIV). And the Lord "hears the prayer of the righteous" (Proverbs 15:29 NIV). So while I don't know exactly what the issue is that you personally are wrestling with, I do know that the promise to us in 1 Peter 3:12 is true, "For the eyes of the Lord are on the righteous and His ears are attentive to their prayer" (NIV).

Wayne Cordeiro, author of *Leading on Empty*, is helpful here when speaking on the need for solitary refinement.

> The desert fathers went to the wilderness because the simplicity of life there offered few distractions. They quieted every demand and opened their hearts to only One Voice. In the silent sands they turned to prayer and reconnection with God. Then when they were refreshed, they'd return to teach, counsel,

make spiritual decisions, and provide pastoral care. In due time, they turned again to the desert for another period of refreshing. This oscillation between the desert and ministry is a nonnegotiable pattern...[92]

Charles H. Spurgeon said, "Quietude, which some men cannot abide because it reveals their inward poverty, is as a palace of cedar to the wise, for along its hallowed courts the King in His beauty deigns to walk."[93]

By now, you get the point. There is a time you must step back and step away, and I would highly encourage us to focus on two very practical areas of our lives that can transform how we live and what we prioritize.

Let Go What You Can't Control

As we know, with maturity comes more responsibility. With wise handling of these responsibilities comes more opportunity. With more opportunities and responsibilities, we accept that we over time become overwhelmed by being overworked. I find it slightly humorous when high school students will tell me just how stressed they are. Now I don't want to minimize that many have lots to juggle with academics, athletics or fine art activities, relationships, and their nine daily hours on social media but the reality is that this time in their life is for most, the least, not the most responsibility they will ever have to manage. Yet, whether working in high school or college, raising families, or leading a large company, we need to understand that there are some things we are engaged in, have supported, or are participating in that frankly are not our responsibility.

Hear me when I say that there is nothing wrong with being engaged and even having some concern for a particular matter. However, what we each have to be able to decipher is what is simply a concern and what my own personal responsibility is that will rise and fall on my shoulders. For each of us, there are things that are asked of us that we must do. These are things we will be evaluated on and held accountable for, and others are expecting that we will come through and make it happen in a specific area. For example, it is my responsibility in my line of work as a principal to hire teachers, evaluate and supervise staff, and ensure that we have a safe and secure campus. Now I might have concerns as to whether students have had a good breakfast before they arrived at school, their parents are taking them to church every Sunday, or students are getting adequate sleep and not playing videos or staying on their cell phones until two in the morning. These are good concerns, but they are not in my immediate sphere of influence or responsibility. For me to try to ensure that parents are taking care of these things with their child would detract and cause me to lose focus on the areas of responsibility that I must accomplish.

Let's go back to where Jesus said, "Let's go somewhere else" in response to the disciple saying, "Everyone is looking for you" (Mark 1:37–38 NIV). Jesus was prioritizing His ministry. He was walking away from healing people's sicknesses and ailments. Of course, the townspeople loved the miracles, and of course Jesus was concerned about the needs of the people, but He had a higher calling and a responsibility that His Father had given to Him, and that is where He needed to place His focus and attention.

Pursue What You Must

So what was it that Jesus was saying yes to that would cause Him to say, "Let's go somewhere else?" In Mark 1:38, Jesus said, "Let us go on to the next towns, that I may preach there also, for that is why I came out" (ESV). In the next chapter, Mark reinforces the focus of Jesus's ministry when we see a very similar situation where the Pharisees are accusing Jesus of eating with the sinners and tax collectors. He replied to them, "It is not the healthy who need a doctor, but the sick. I have not come to call the righteous, but sinners" (Mark 2:17 NIV).

Jesus was very intentional about why He had come to earth and was intent on fulfilling His mission. In John 6:38, Jesus says, "For I have come down from heaven, not to do my own will but to do the will of him who sent me" (NIV). Jesus, one of the Trinity, is on a mission from God to rescue us for God. He knew that, left to ourselves, we would receive the full wrath of God, so He stops doing really good work to focus on the best work, the most important work that only He could accomplish.

This whole idea is not only freeing that we don't have to run around trying to save the world, but it also provides great clarity and direction for us. Jesus could have done anything He wanted, and it would have been really good. However, He came for two main reasons:

1. To seek and to save and rescue the lost (Mark 2:17; Luke 19:5, 9–10; Isaiah 61:1–3)
2. To die as an atoning sacrifice for the sins of the lost so they might have eternal life (John 12:24–27; John 3:16)

Here, Jesus modeled for us what it meant to stay on mission, remained focused, and do those things that only He could do. So what about you? What is really important that only you can do and only you must do? Despite what most of us think, about 75 percent of our jobs can be done by many others. (I understand this is not a universal truth.) About another 15 percent of what we do someone with the right training that goes through a good interview selection process could be our replacement, and very little would change. However, there is about 10 percent that we do what no one else can do. So what is that? Here is where Tim McGraw's song "Live Like You Were Dying" is likely pretty helpful.

Faced with eternity suddenly makes what is important—what is most important—come rushing to the forefront. Staring eternity in the face also makes not the what but the who most important come shining through with vivid colors. If you have ever had surgery or been in a serious accident that requires surgery, those who came to see you start to make your shortlist of just who is most important. Reflect on your creed you wrote. If done well, this will resonate with your soul when you consider what it means to make eternal investments.

In the spring of 2019, my seventy-nine-year-old father fell off a twenty-five-foot roof and shattered his femur. He broke it in several other places near the hip and cracked some ribs. It is only by the grace of God that he is still alive from such a fall. However, it was our immediate family, a few friends, and select church members who came around to visit him. Such is the case in such events as we affirm our love, affirmation, and affection for each other.

Wayne Cordeiro talks of how Bryan Dyson, the former COO of Coca-Cola, delivered the commencement address at Georgia Tech in 1996. There he tried to explain the distinction of what is most important in life,

> Imagine life as a game in which you are juggling some five balls in the air. You name them—work, family, health, friends, and spirit—and you are keeping all of these in the air. You will soon understand that work is a rubber ball. If you drop it, it will bounce back. But the other four balls—family, health, friends and spirit—are made of glass. If you drop one of these they will be irrevocably scuffed, marked, nicked, damaged, or even shattered. They will never be the same. You must understand that and strive for balance in your life.[94]

At the center of Jesus's intentional mission was deep intimate relationships. Don't compromise your family and close friends under the guise of a divine calling. These relationships are not separate from your calling and life mission; rather they are at the center, the very core of it.

Here is what I know, and here is where I have been working to put more of my focus and priorities. Notice I say this in the present tense as this all is a work-in-progress for me:

1. Having daily communion with Jesus in prayer and His word
2. Pursuing my wife like I did back in the early 1990s
3. Leading my family where Scripture is preeminent and Jesus is the standard
4. Living and leading from a gospel orientation at my work (school) where Jesus shines through, even in my messes
5. Being physically active and pursuing interests outside of work, like writing and the great outdoors

Life on Purpose Restored and Renewed

So you might be asking, "So what does all this have to do with courage?" Everything! It begins with the courage to say "no" to certain things, even good things. Of course, it is one thing to acknowledge what to say "no" to and another to actually carry it out. This word is simpler to say than to actually carry this out. Yet, if you are able to follow the model that Jesus set for us and step away from the good to pick up the most important and those things that align your life purpose and calling, it will lead you toward a life restored, renewed, and on purpose. So have the courage to say "no" as well as the courage to say "yes" and then to follow through with your life priorities. This courage challenge is crucial. As you consider what God has entrusted to you to steward, lead, and care for, I suspect that you too will be able to identify those vital areas you must identify and pursue.

Courage Challenge

1. Identify those areas in your life that have been concerns and consumed your time and thoughts and that frankly are not your responsibility. Write them down and consciously decide to disengage from these areas that are outside your control and consuming your limited resources. Maybe they need to be minimized or even eliminated. The higher these were elevated in your life, the more difficult and the more assistance you may need to root out or tear down what well could be an idol in your life.

2. Identify those areas in your life that are the 10 percent that only you can do and must do. For these areas, you are the lead role, the main character, and the show can barely go on if you don't show up in these vital areas. Identity them and then begin to prioritize them in your schedule. Everyone has only twenty-four hours in a day. It is how we use those hours. So either you or others manage your schedule.

3. Finally create two columns and identify those areas in your life that give life and those areas that take life from you. If like most, your daily list of those things that take or drain life is usually longer than the list that describes the activities that give life. Again, this comes back to schedule. Identifying life-giving activities is critical, but it does us no good if we never do them and only sit longingly gazing at the much-desired list wishing that we weren't so busy. Choose life and pursue those areas that fill your tank and renew, refresh, reinvigorate, and restore the life that God has intended and given for us to live. (Despite having somewhat of a desk job, I can't sit behind it long without having to interact and engage with people, get active and participate in athletics, exercise, hike, or go on walks with my wife. I enjoy writing, but it took me four long years to finally finish this book as I took many months off at a time.) Find what gives and breathes life back

into you and make sure these are scheduled into part of your day and then guard and defend these life-giving moments, events, and activities and do not let other things creep in to seize that ground that you have just reclaimed. Once you have the high ground, it is your job to defend it from other suitors wishing to take it from you. I know full well that many well-intentioned people and causes will clamor for your time and attention. There must be some ground where no compromising and no conceding takes place. You have taken the high ground like a well-trained soldier. Fight for it and do not surrender what you have rightfully and appropriately claimed. Stand To!

CHAPTER THIRTEEN

LEAD WITH CONVICTION

*Not only in word, but also in power and in the
Holy Spirit and with full conviction.*
—1 THESSALONIANS 1:5 (ESV)

Always stand on principle ... even if you stand alone.
—JOHN ADAMS

You can't endure in bearing fruit if you sever the root.
—WILLIAM WILBERFORCE

Here I Stand

In the 1500s, a man by the name of Martin Luther, an Augustinian monk, once stood alone in front of the most powerful, influential, elite dignitaries in the world, but he stood on a principle that would change his life and the rest of the world forever. He read in Scripture from Romans 1:17 that "The righteous shall live by faith."

These six words shocked Luther because up to that point, he had come to believe that it was his good works that justified him as being good. Yet when he was introduced to this alien righteousness that belonged to someone else, for something He did, namely Christ, it led him to say, "When I discovered that, I was born again of the Holy Ghost. And the doors of paradise swung open, I walked through."[95]

This deep biblical conviction led him to dig deep both into God's Word and to hold it up against the current practices held by the Roman Catholic Church of the 1500s. Concerned and troubled by the differences he saw in Scripture and these church practices, he penned his complaints in what has been known as the *95 Theses* and then nailed them to the church door of Wittenburg, Germany, on October 31, 1517. Now over five hundred years later, which not only were his actions he took against the church, it was his deeply held convictions to remain steadfast and unmovable despite intense pressure to back down and recant from his position. As he stood at the Diet (Assembly) of Worms in 1521 before powerful clergy and statesmen, he stood alone with his conscience bound by scripture and said, "Unless I am convicted by Scripture and plain reason (I do not accept the authority of popes and councils because they have contradicted each other), my conscience is captive to the Word of God. I cannot and will not recant anything, for to go against conscience is neither right nor safe. So help me God. Amen."

Luther's collected works, issued later under his supervision, give the closing words as, "Here I stand, I can do no other, so help me God. Amen." [96] That version of his speech has come down so memorably to posterity.

Colliding Worldviews

When a Christian is guided by God and His Word, he knows truth and the standard for absolute truth. God reveals Himself and His will to us personally through His Word. Yet a culture devoid of God's Word is guided by personal opinions, feelings, emotions, and personal beliefs that have the individual as the originator and supreme authority. Such a worldview is like an ocean with no floor or a buffet with only side dishes and no meat for substances. When one holds to biblical objective truth and the secular humanist believes reality is subjective with truth found from within oneself, such a standoff, as is recorded with Martin Luther and the Roman Catholic Church, of the 1500s is inevitable.

Conviction Clarification

It is important to first understand what a biblical conviction is in contrast to a personal conviction. A true biblical conviction is more than just to accept something as truth, for to stop there can lead one to act as judge of others. In addition, biblical convictions cannot be defined merely as personal behaviors, for to do so would lead us to self-justification of our actions. Instead true biblical conviction is these two ideas wed together as it represents truths that change and motivate our daily behavior.

To look at the story of Luther, it was the truth from God's Word that the righteous or the just will live by faith, and it is not of man's works that they earn their way to heaven that caused him to not just take the action he took but to take the stand under great pressure to recant.

Can you imagine how bold Luther was to literally get a hammer and a nail and take his ninety-five grievances and actually nail it to a church door? This goes to the very essence of this book title, *Stand To: Finding Masculine Courage in a Stand-Down World*. Standing down was not something Martin Luther was willing or ready to ever do!

Without a doubt, a personal conviction can be or can originate from a biblical conviction, but the wording alone convolutes the meaning and can lead down a slippery slope as thinking fluctuates based on emotions, opinions, circumstances, who is around, and what one is feeling. As Dorothy Sayers once said, "In the world it is called Tolerance, but in hell it is called Despair ... the sin that believes in nothing, cares for nothing, seeks to know nothing, interferes with nothing, enjoys nothing, hates nothing, finds purpose in nothing, lives for nothing, and remains alive because there is nothing for which it will die."[97]

Conviction-less

By way of contrast, those without biblical convictions are prone to be easily influenced and manipulated and struggle with making solid decisions. Look at what Scripture has to say,

- Indecisive: "But when he asks, he must believe and not doubt, because he who doubts is like a wave of the sea, blown and tossed by the wind. That man should not think he will receive anything from the Lord; he is double-minded, unstable in all he does" (James 1:6-8 NIV). Such a person as described in James has a hard time making decisions and is constantly second-guessing themselves as they lack the anchor to ground them and guide their decisions.
- Immature: "Then we will no longer be infants, tossed back and forth by the waves, and blown here and there by every wind of teaching and by the cunning and craftiness of men in their deceitful scheming. Instead, speaking the truth in love, we will in all things grow who is the Head, that is, Christ" (Ephesians 4:14–15 NIV). Lacking deep biblical conviction roots make it easy for such a person to be easily moved and convinced to take a different position because of their lack of grounding.
- Hypocritical: "Woe to you, teachers of the law and Pharisees, you hypocrites! You clean the outside of the cup and dish, but inside they are full of greed and self-indulgence" (Matthew 23:25 NIV). The focus of such a person is not from a deeply held conviction, but instead the opinion of others is far more valuable, and so the external performance in front of others is more important than the internal moral compass guided by God and His Word. Such a person will easily say and do

things for the approval of others and not be well respected for such an inconsistent life pattern.

Best Leaders Have Conviction

It is not hard to see that to effectively lead others, the person who is not well-grounded and is indecisive, immature, and hypocritical will be unfit and unequipped to lead anyone for any significant amount of time. In 2016, *Forbes* ran an article entitled "Why The Best Leaders Have Conviction." Author Travis Bradberry writes,

> Conviction in a leader is an incredibly valuable yet increasingly rare trait. It's in short supply because our brains are wired to overreact to uncertainty with fear. As uncertainty increases, the brain shifts control over to the limbic system, the place where emotions, such as anxiety and panic, are generated. We crave certainty. Our brains are so geared up for certainty that our subconscious can monitor and store over two million data points, which the brain uses to predict the future. And that isn't just a neat little side trick— it's the primary purpose of the neocortex, which is 76% of the brain's total mass … Our brains reward us for certainty … In business, things change so quickly that there's a great deal of uncertainty about what's going to happen next month, let alone next year. And uncertainty takes up a lot of people's mental energy and makes them less effective at their jobs.
>
> The brain perceives uncertainty as a threat, which sparks the release of cortisol, a stress hormone that disrupts memory, depresses the immune system, and increases the risk of high blood pressure and depression. These are things no leader wants his or her team to endure.

Leaders with conviction create an environment of certainty for everyone. When a leader is absolutely convinced that he's chosen the best course of action, everyone who follows him unconsciously absorbs this belief and the accompanying emotional state. Mirror neurons are responsible for this involuntary response. They mirror the emotional states of other people—especially those we look to for guidance. This ensures that leaders with conviction put us at ease.

Leaders with conviction show us that the future is certain and that we're all headed in the right direction. Their certainty is neurologically shared by everyone … When leaders have conviction, people's brains can relax, so to speak, letting them concentrate on what needs to be done. When people feel more secure in the future, they're happier and produce higher quality work.[98]

Hanging Out with Jesus

Al Mohler in an article "Leading with Conviction," writes,

> When the leader walks into the room, a passion for truth had better enter with him. Authentic leadership does not emerge out of a vacuum. The leadership that matters most is convictional—deeply convictional … We believe the gospel, and we have faith in Christ. Our beliefs have substance and our faith has an object … We live out of these truths and are willing to die for these truths.[99]

Recall the scene after Peter and John, two apostles, who just after Jesus's death and resurrection had the courage to challenge the Sanhedrin and defy their order to not preach in the public about

Jesus. However, Peter and John had some real concerns as they said in Acts 4. In fact, check out Peter's response to his accusers,

> If we are being examined today concerning a good deed done to a crippled man, by what means this man has been healed, let it be known to all of you and to all the people of Israel that by the name of Jesus Christ of Nazareth, whom you crucified, whom God raised from the dead—by him this man is standing before you well. This Jesus is the stone that was rejected by you, the builders, which has become the cornerstone. And there is salvation in no one else, for there is no other name under heaven given among men by which we must be saved. (Acts 4:8–12 ESV)

But check out the response in the following verses, "Now when they saw the boldness of Peter and John, and perceived that they were uneducated, common men, they were astonished. And they recognized that they had been with Jesus" (Acts 4:13 ESV).

Truth + Conviction = Leadership

What a powerful last verse! How is it that Peter was able to challenge the Sanhedrin, to speak so boldly, and to even accuse them of what they did to Jesus? Each phrase he speaks is like one punch after another squarely landed by the heavyweight champion of the world as point after point is driven home with precise accuracy. The response of the people says it all. They saw that there was nothing special about these men. In fact, they were normal, common guys who were uneducated, but—and here it is—"they have been with Jesus." Did Peter have a deeply held conviction in the person and work of Jesus Christ? You better believe he did.

In Acts 4:20, "for we cannot but speak of what we have seen and heard" (ESV). Peter was so convinced of his message that he was willing to die for it, and that is exactly what happened. In fact, when it came time for him to be crucified, he had one request, to be crucified upside down because he felt unworthy to die the same death as Jesus. There is no doubt Peter was committed and convinced and held a deep conviction of who Jesus was. Yet we must not look to Peter as the focal point of this story but instead look to and believe in the eternal truth that God had revealed to him, Jesus is the Son of God and his Lord and his Savior. This deep biblical conviction is what is most important and should not be missed.

Al Mohler adds,

> We cannot lead in a way that is faithful to Christ and effective for Christ's people if we are not deeply invested in Christian truth. We cannot faithfully lead if we do not first faithfully believe—and if we are not deeply committed to Christian truth … The starting point for Christian leadership is not the leader but the eternal truths that God has revealed to us—the truths that allow the world to make sense to us, frame our understandings, and propel us to action.[100]

This is why the apostle Paul encouraged the Thessalonians to know that the gospel had come to them, "not only in word, but also in power and in the Holy Spirit and with full conviction" (1 Thessalonians 1:5 ESV).

Hard Decisions Made Easy

Men with conviction are admired when they are standing upright when the wind blows the strongest and fiercest. When leaders make hard decisions in difficult times, people wonder how they could decide either so quickly or be able to figure out what to do when the pressure is turned up and when under such urgency they are compelled to respond. Thankfully we have a great example of not necessarily the man, extraordinary though he may be, but a principle for us to follow. I will simply call it the Daniel Principle that we find in Daniel 1:5–7.

We see three things are assigned to Daniel in this passage that are going to be completely different from his upbringing as an Israelite. He was to be given a new name, he was to be educated in the literature and language of the Chaldeans, and he was assigned to eat the king's food (meat) and wine. For a young man like Daniel who had studied the Scriptures, I am sure he preferred his Jewish name and his Jewish education, but neither of these was necessarily sinful.

However, when it came to eating the king's meat and drinking the king's wine, he knew that was not permissible according to Scripture. He knew in Leviticus 11:4–20 that God had prohibited the eating of unclean meat that had been offered to idols and that in Proverbs 23:31–35 it counsels against drinking intoxicating wine.

So when this was placed before him, Daniel had already decided what he was going to do. In Daniel 1:8 we read, "But Daniel resolved that he would not defile himself with the king's food or with the wine that he drank" (ESV). The word *resolved* means to be "firmly determined to do something." Due to Daniel's convictions, he had already pre-determined or decided that he was not going to be taking part in the king's meat and drink. This was an easy decision for Daniel. His convictions led, and his actions followed.

We know the devil seeks to wear us down very gradually where the giving in is ever so slight, but over time the effects are massive. C. S. Lewis nails this point in *The Screwtape Letters* where the demon Screwtape is mentoring his nephew Wormwood on how to slowly and gradually disrupt good kingdom work from happening when he says, "Indeed the safest road to Hell is the gradual one—the gentle slope, soft underfoot, without sudden turning, without milestones, without signposts."[101]

A bold and courageous activist in history who came under great attack was William Wilberforce, who sought to abolish the slave trade in England. In the book *Mission Drift*, its authors speak of the magnitude Wilberforce attempted to accomplish when they write, the cause would threaten the very foundation of the British Empire, through campaigning for a cause that would disrupt Britain's financial power and their global position, but he also went practically blind, suffered from ulcerated bowels, became addicted to doctor-prescribed opium, and his spine was so curved he needed a brace to keep his head from resting on his chest. Wilberforce was a man with a cause. But much more importantly, he was a man with a foundation. He stated, "You can't endure in bearing fruit if you sever the root." The root for him was a firmly held belief in God's atoning work on the cross and a lifetime of spiritual disciplines.[102]

Wilberforce knew that for him to take on the cause that he was to tackle, the convictions of who he was before God and the inherent dignity, worth, and value of all men created equal before God would be the foundational convictions he would unswervingly hold to, despite his physical ailments and all the noise and clamor around him seeking to pull him down.

Wilberforce understood that what he was up against was way, way bigger than he was, and for him to take on an entire nation, this was going to have to come from something and someone far superior than him. We see the answer in John 15:4–5 where Jesus says, "Abide in me, and I in you. As the branch cannot bear fruit by itself, unless it abides in the vine, neither can you, unless you abide in me. I am the vine; you are the branches. Whoever abides in me and I in him, he it is that bears much fruit, for apart from me you can do nothing" (ESV).

To deeply abide in Christ must be the very foundation of a convictional leader. Dr. Arnold Cook wrote these words in *Historical Drift*, "A weakened commitment to Scripture, more than any other factor, has facilitated historical drift. It renders us vulnerable to the subtle accommodation to culture."[103]

This is why when the children of Israel were receiving the law from God, we see in Deuteronomy how God was instructive in how they were to constantly keep God's word in front of them. In Deuteronomy 6:6–9 (NIV), we read,

> These commandments that I give to you today are to be on your hearts. Impress them on your children. Talk about them when you sit at home and when you walk along the road, when you lie down and when you get up. Tie them as symbols on your hands and bind them on your foreheads. Write them on the doorframe of your houses and on your gates.

In summary, talk about God's Word constantly, keep it in front of you, and make sure your children know this also. The temptation to give in to the other nation's gods and practices was literally just around the corner. They knew they were one generation away from being a pagan nation cut off from God's blessing.

Anarchy in Seattle

There is nothing easy about leading with conviction, particularly when we now live in a world where pretty much anything goes and is up to personal interpretation and subsequent action. In the tensions that captured the attention of our entire nation following the death of George Floyd during the summer of 2020, we saw one decision after another being based on reaction and emotion as stores and vehicles were burned, there was a cry for defunding police, and even no-police zones and a section of downtown Seattle was overrun by anarchists who wanted to serve as their own law as violence, thievery, destruction, and anarchy raged. They took over an area of downtown Seattle that they initially called CHAZ, or Capitol Hill Autonomous Zone, where the police were barred from entering.

The shocking part of it all was that the local authorities permitted it. Meanwhile, those who lived or had businesses within that zone were terrified as it was anything but safe if the mob chose to attack a person or to storm and deface a business. Without police presence, some within CHAZ had been shot and killed. However, we shouldn't be surprised at such things, for when men will elevate themselves to the highest authority and are unwilling to surrender to godly principles, values, and morals, anarchy will ensure.

Steps to Leading with Conviction

However, consider the juxtaposition of following these five godly leadership principles that would cause one to be a leader guided and directed by God-honoring convictions.

1. Have a deep and abiding dependence upon God and His Word
2. Embrace biblical convictions that will be your firm foundation
3. Hold unwavering to these convictions through a disciplined life
4. Decide in advance, like Daniel, as life choices flow from your convictions
5. Hold every thought captive to the obedience of Christ

Our mind leads our bodies into action. Deliberately determine those thoughts that will dominate or take residence in your mind. Reject and dismiss what seeks to prey upon your convictions and lead you astray.

Convictions to the Death

Let me end with a story that took place back in the 1500s. Queen Mary had ascended the throne of England in 1553, and it didn't take long for her to put to death at least two hundred people for their religious convictions, earning her the name "Bloody Mary." The godliness of many of her victims made them stand out. Two such men were Nicholas Ridley and Hugh Latimer. Ridley had been a chaplain; Hugh Latimer also became an influential preacher. These men were loved by their congregations and were students of God's Word.

When Ridley was asked if he believed the pope was heir to the authority of Peter as the foundation of the church, he replied that the church was not built on any man but on the truth Peter confessed, that Christ was the Son of God. Ridley said he could not honor the pope in Rome since the papacy was seeking its own glory, not the glory of God.

Latimer told the church commissioners, "Christ made one oblation and sacrifice for the sins of the whole world, and that a perfect sacrifice; neither needeth there to be, nor can there be, any other propitiatory sacrifice."

Such statements caused them to fall out of grace from the church and the throne, and on October 16, 1555, they were burned at the stake while tied back to back. As Ridley was being tied to the stake, he prayed, "Oh, heavenly Father, I give unto thee most hearty thanks that thou hast called me to be a professor of thee, even unto death. I beseech thee, Lord God, have mercy on this realm of England, and deliver it from all her enemies."

As the flames quickly rose, Latimer encouraged Ridley, "Be of good comfort, Mr. Ridley, and play the man! We shall this day light such a candle by God's grace, in England, as I trust never shall be put out."[104]

Courage Challenge

You have been given many examples of men who have stood tall in adversity and had the courage to act when others remained speechless or succumbed to the pressure around them. This courage challenge will be twofold and get at the very heart of who you are. Thomas

Jefferson asked, "Do you want to know who you are? Don't ask. Act! Action will delineate and define you."

1. Identify the top three areas where you struggle to live from a place of biblical conviction. I am not asking or questioning what you believe, but instead whether you practically have the discipline to live out or practice these biblical convictions. For instance, you might believe it is biblically wrong to lust after a woman, and yet you regularly struggle with viewing pornography. That would be a disconnect between your convictions and your actions. Another example might be your desire to be a truth-teller, and yet you find that to your boss at work you are constantly giving partial truths or presenting a perspective that makes you look better than your actual performance. If you feel inclined, by all means list more than three but focus on the three primary areas where you find there is the greatest disconnect between what you believe (convictions) and what you do (actions). This is a normal struggle as Paul said in Romans 7:15, "for I do not understand what I do. For what I want to do I do not do, but what I hate I do" (NIV).

2. Identify the top five guiding biblical convictions that you would want your life to be marked as having modeled. For example, if I mention the name Abraham Lincoln, you should quickly be thinking of honesty for "Honest Abe." If I mention Martin Luther King, Jr., you might quickly think of peace or nonviolent protests. If you think of Mother Theresa, you might think of compassion or service. What about you? When your name is mentioned, what are those guiding biblical convictions that those who know you would be able to say about you? If you are struggling with this, maybe ask those closest to you. If they struggle to answer you, it just might be that you have not been living and leading courageously from a place of biblical conviction. It is never too late to begin. So whether this is an easy task for you or you are possibly

beginning with a clean slate, take time to identify those top five biblical convictions that you want your life to be marked by when your closing breaths are taken knowing you have lived a godly life of significance before others and you have run the race and finished well.

Band of Brothers Leadership

A real-life example of a battle-tested warrior who saw leading with conviction of character and moral courage is WWII war hero Major Dick Winters from East Company, 506th Parachute Infantry Regiment 101st Airborne Division, from which was created the HBO movie series, *Band of Brothers*. Major Dick Winters, who daily was in the stand to position, ends his book, *Beyond Band of Brothers - The War Memoirs of Major Dick Winters* by reflecting on leadership. In fact, before Steve Ambrose passed away in 2003, he told Major Winters, "From now on, Winters, if you are going to talk about anything, talk about leadership!" On the very last page of his nearly three hundred-page book, he lists ten principles for success entitled "Leadership at the Point of the Bayonet." Notice how many of these have to do with the need to possess and live from deep conviction.

1.   Strive to be a leader of character, competence, and courage.
2.   Lead from the front. Say, "Follow me!" and then lead the way.
3.   Stay in top physical shape—physical stamina is the root of mental toughness.
4.   Develop your team. If you know your people, are setting realistic goals and expectations, and lead by example, you will develop teamwork.
5.   Delegate responsibility to your subordinates and let them do their jobs. You can't do a good job if you don't have a chance to use your imagination or your creativity.

6. Anticipate problems and prepare to overcome obstacles. Don't wait until you get to the top of the ridge and then make up your mind.

7. Remain humble. Don't worry about who receives the credit. Never let people or authority go to your head.

8. Take a moment of self-reflection. Look at yourself in the mirror every night and ask yourself if you did your best.

9. True satisfaction comes from getting the job done. The key to a successful leader is to earn respect - not because of rank or position, but because you are a leader of character.

10. Hang tough! - Never, ever, give up![105]

CHAPTER FOURTEEN

STRONG TO THE FINISH

*I have fought the good fight, I have finished
the course, I have kept the faith.*
—2 TIMOTHY 4:7 (NIV)

Hang tough!—Never, ever, give up![106]
—DICK WINTERS, *BAND OF BROTHERS*

Move the Line

We missed the championship again?! This is what my high school boys' soccer team felt after finishing back-to-back state runner-ups in 2017 and 2018. In 2018 we had won twenty-one consecutive games and just felt as though we were destined to win the elusive state championship we had let slip through our hands in 2017. However, that was not to be the case. Both were crushing defeats for the boys, and so when the 2019 season rolled around, it became our aim to focus on how we would finish each challenge before us. We knew the pressure was going to be on us as we began the year being ranked number one in the state and after two years of being at the top. We had a huge bull's-eye on our back. In practice, the players regularly heard me say, "Move the line."

What I meant by that was anytime we were doing fitness running,

I didn't want the boys running to the line as the final destination, but through the line. The finish line was supposed to be part of the journey. We mentally were working with the boys to not simply focus on getting to the line but to accelerate and explode through the line and to create an imaginary line five to ten yards beyond the actual finish line.

The boys started to catch on and would set goals and challenge themselves beyond what I was even trying to establish with them. For example, at one point they realized that the state record for consecutive shutouts was nine. After we were at five in a row, they set out to eliminate shots from the opponents and worked extra hard on the defensive end of the ball to see if we could actually break that record. I was amazed at their willingness and desire to move the line in the little things, and so when shut out ninth and tenth in a row came against teams that I felt were superior to us, I was not surprised when they broke that state record.

As we pressed toward the state championship, I could tell before we took the field for the 2019 state championship that we were now a team that had learned to move the line and to finish strong. In fact, we had pre-game T-shirts made for our guys that said "Finish Strong" with 2 Timothy 4:7 printed on it. We knew we were going to finish the season; everyone does. Some finish a season with great regret and often sadness and tears if they end with a loss, while others are content to do just a little better than last year. Regardless, every season comes to a close, the lingering question was how we were going to finish the season.

On May 13, 2019, it was clear this team meant business. The night before they had won the semifinal game 2–1 after having gone to overtime, sudden death and a penalty shoot-out where all five of our guys taking penalty kicks made to them earn a third consecutive trip to the state championship. Even the preparation for that moment can hardly be replicated in the training with the pressure of the playoff game on the line. However, each player stated after the game that they felt peace stepping to the ball as they rifled it past the goalkeeper.

From the first whistle of the state championship match, the boys were clearly on a mission and not to be denied this time. Within twenty minutes, we were already winning 3-0, and as the final second ticked off the clock, the team had won 5-0 and earned the right to hoist the state championship trophy over their heads. As they learned to move the line, they saw the total effect it had on what it meant to finish strong and to conclude the year as they started, the number-one 5A team in the state of Alabama and sixteenth in the nation!

It is my sincere hope that these sixteen- to nineteen-year-old men will recall the lessons they have learned on the soccer field and to apply these life principles of being a finisher at whatever the Lord calls them to do and to be a part of. As the apostle Paul's life is drawing to a close, we see in 2 Timothy 4:7 him being able to declare that he is a finisher in the race and the tasks that the Lord had entrusted to him.

Sent to Finish

This reminds me of John Stephen Akhwari, the marathon Olympian from Tanzania, sent to Mexico City to represent his country in the 1968 Summer Olympic Games. John understood the importance of finishing even when people around him and the circumstances called for him to drop out of the race and to just give up.

> Unfortunately, Akhwari suffered a fall during the race. And it wasn't a gentle tumble on a grassy knoll. He fell hard on rough concrete, badly cutting his right leg and dislocating his knee. Medical personnel arrived quickly and bandaged his wounds. But the dislocated knee required more treatment than they could provide in the city streets. He needed to go to the hospital. But against their advice, Akhwari instead stood up and started down the road behind the rest of the runners.
>
> Given the severity of his injuries, he couldn't run his normal pace. With a combination of jogging, hobbling, and walking, he pushed ahead. At 2:20:26

into the race, Mamo Walde of Ethiopia crossed the finish line in first place. Most of the remaining competitors finished within a few minutes. Akhwari was nowhere close.

An hour later, the Olympic stadium had only a few thousand people left in it. The marathon was the last event of the day, and the sun had already set. Mexico City was brutal on the marathon runners. At over 7,400 feet in altitude, the air has 23 percent less oxygen than at sea level. As a result, 17 of the 74 runners failed to finish the race that day. Akhwari, bloodied and injured, was determined to not be one of them. Followed by a police escort, and clearly, in great pain, Akhwari finally arrived and limped his way onto the track, his loosening bandages dangling from his leg. As the diminished crowd cheered in awe and disbelief, John Stephen Akhwari made his way around the track and crossed the finish line at 3:25:27, in the last place. The few remaining reporters rushed onto the field to ask him why he continued running in his condition. He responded simply, "My country didn't send me 5,000 miles to start this race. They sent me 5,000 miles to finish it."[107]

As we consider what it means to finish strong, the words of George Washington Carver offer us direction for our personal lives, "No individual has any right to come into this world and go out of it without leaving behind distinct and legitimate reason for having passed through it." It is interesting when we look at the Bible and the dig into 347 biographies recorded there for us. Surprisingly, what Scripture tells us is that only 67 actually finished strong. This ought to get our attention and cause us to wonder why less than 20 percent of all these biographical sketches recorded in the Bible were able to remain faithful and finish strong.

Weak Finishers

Recently I was talking to a good friend who shared an experience he had where his college soccer teammates wanted to get back together for a bit of a reunion and head to Colorado for a ski trip. It didn't take long for him to realize that despite all attending the same Christian college and playing for the same Christian coach, many of his former teammates had dropped out of the race. The language and conversations were ungodly and disheartening to my friend to the point where he had to say, "Hey, guys, I can't be part of these conversations as they just are not reflective of where I am in life and don't find them honoring to the Lord."

That started other conversations with some of the guys where one specifically commented, "I just found living the Christian life too hard, and I gave up on it."

My friend came away from the trip saddened to see that these guys who shared much in common in college had drifted away to where they no longer were even interested in pursuing a life honoring to Christ. So how does this happen? Let's look at a case study in the life of Reheboam in 1 Kings 12 as his story sadly is reflected in too many men today. Reheboam was the son of King Solomon and the grandson of King David. While both his father and grandfather made mistakes, he also had the opportunity to see some incredible examples to follow as a king. Very few have such legacies to observe and follow as his own dad was the wisest man on earth and his grandfather was known as a man after God's own heart. Despite all this, he failed miserably and here is why.

1. He ignored God's Word. When he became king, the people wanted to know if he would be kinder or harsher than his father in how he dealt with them. Instead of seeking the Lord and consulting God's Word, he asked counselors around him. When the older and wiser men gave him counsel he didn't want to hear, he found younger counselors with whom he had grown up, who told him what he wanted to hear and to be

more oppressive to his people. *Question: Do I regularly seek God's Word and will in my life?*

2. He ignored his own father's legacy. Naturally it must have been tough to have followed the wisest man in the world, and yet his father also made some significant mistakes. Every man has to reflect on his own father's legacy and how he is/ has finished the race marked before him. What should be pursued, dropped, changed, adjusted, or renewed? Sons get a front-row seat, for better or worse, to consider the legacy they have received. It is handed down to them and will be theirs to continue. The question is whether they will finish strong and embrace a godly legacy that may be generational or possibly even be a first generation pursuing a strong godly finish. *Question: What have I or what do I need to learn from my father?*

3. He ignored wise counsel. For Reheboam, there was not a void of wise counsel. Instead it was a simple rejection of the wisdom provided to him by the seasoned counselors in his life. Stubborn and prideful, he decided to ignore counsel that would have saved his throne, life, and legacy. *Question: Do I seek and listen to wise godly counsel even if I don't like what they have to say to me?*

4. He listened to "yes men" in his life. When he didn't hear what he wanted to hear from the older wiser counselors in his life, he sought counsel from his childhood friends, who told him what he wanted to hear. He allowed poor influences to enter his life instead of the wisdom and instruction of those who would provide godly direction that would help him be a strong leader and finisher. *Question: Are my closest friends having a positive influence on me or just telling me what I want to hear?*

5. He neglected his own legacy. As Reheboam lived for the moment, he failed to consider how his current actions would affect those around him. As a king, his influence was great, and his nation, family, son, and legacy would be affected. And they were … adversely. His nation fell into deeper sin, and his

own son became an even more prolific sinner. Thousands of years later, Reheboam's poor legacy remains recorded for all to read about in God's Word. *Question: Would I want those around me, those who follow behind me, those of whom I dearly love, to repeat my life example?*

Reality Check

When it comes to whether or not we will leave a legacy, this is one of those areas we have no control over. Every single person will leave a legacy without a doubt. The question is what kind of legacy we will be leaving and what impact we will have on those we leave behind. You might feel you are on track or are wildly off track. As it is said in an athletic contest, it is not how you start but how you end that matters. We have recorded for us in Scripture the legacy of the thief on the cross who had led a life as a crook, and yet his dying moment and final words are recorded for us in Scripture as his legacy goes down as defending Jesus on the cross and asking the Savior of the world to remember him when he goes to heaven, as he acknowledges the truth of Jesus's lordship!

To finish strong does not happen by accident, and it is never the path of least resistance. Consider the opening story of my soccer team and the difficulties, obstacles, and setbacks from previous years, and yet the resistance to quit and slack off was overcome with resilience to fight through and persevere to the end. This is life, and this is the challenge every one of us must face as we consider how we might fight to the end, stand firm in our faith, and finish the race marked before us.

As an educator, I see the societal focus and even pressure that is amplified and reinforced by parents toward their high school graduates to be highly successful. Practically, this means to get good grades and a good ACT or SAT score, to get into a good college, to get a good job, and to settle down and live a comfortable, successful life.

But what if success is the wrong goal? What if the goal of finishing strong is defined by significance? What if our purpose never was to "have and to hold" but to "give and to serve"?

After all, how should we judge the impact of a person's life? Do we base it on the quality of one life touched or the quantity of lives touched? And when should we measure this, when one is forty, sixty-five, or ninety? Does history make its judgment at ten, one hundred, or one thousand years after a person is gone? And who should determine our life's value and worth? These are important questions for our identity and pursued legacy. Will it be determined by how the most important person in our life views us? Who is the most important person in our lives? If we think about this for a moment, we need to ask ourselves what moves us to action—good or bad or right or wrong? Our answer to this question will help to determine our life's focus, our trajectory, how we spend our time, and eventually our life legacy. If our audience with whom we primarily seek approval is from anyone other than Jesus Christ, how we finish may well compromise our trajectory and legacy for a strong spiritual legacy.

A Strong Finisher

Hopefully you will begin to see things begin to come together from what you read earlier as you worked to establish your life purpose, mission, and trajectory.

1. Coram Deo: To finish strong is the idea of Coram Deo or always living before the presence of God. Under the authority of God and to the glory of God must be the preeminent theme that resonates in our lives. To do so is to understand that we are always under the gaze of our King. He is always watching and knows our thoughts and motives. We also must remember that He is sovereign and to live under this rule and reign extends beyond submission to God but to actively offer our very lives as a sacrifice to Him out of faithful obedience and

deep gratitude. So whatever the Lord calls us to, we are to do so from a deeply spiritual and sacred place, believing and trusting that all of life is sacred and we are not to compartmentalize some aspect as not falling under the lordship of Christ. It all belongs to Him! Next to this idea of Coram Deo, every other idea, goal, or ambition becomes relatively small in comparison and should not hold an equal platitude of significance both in time designated and focus applied.

2. Stay on Course: Go back to your life creed that you wrote. Like a mission statement, this is not something to merely hang on a wall in an office, but it is the measuring stick whereby you evaluate your life actions, aspirations, hopes, and dreams. Are you drifting from this life creed that you set, or is there consistency and a parallel between what you said and what you are doing? In a word, are you being faithful? Subtle drifting or sliding in the moment is often not recognizable. However, over time, the ramifications have the possibility to be irreversible. Think about it: After traveling 100 yards, one degree will lead you 5.2 feet off course. This is not a huge difference. After a mile, you'll be off 92.2 feet. Starting to see the difference maybe? If going from San Francisco to L.A., you would be off by six miles. If traveling around the globe from Washington DC, you'd miss DC by 435 miles and end up in Boston. Now are you getting it? Not even close! In a rocket going to the moon, you'd be 4,169 miles off, nearly twice the diameter of the moon! A daily decision to compromise in an area, no one would ever know, and it would appear to be of no consequence, yet you will surely be missing your mark. A life of tweaking, adjusting, and compromising does not take too long before your course has been rerouted and your final destination has been completely compromised. For example, few people wake up one morning and say, "Today is the day I am going to cheat on my wife," "Today I am going to become addicted to alcohol," or "Today I am going to neglect my wife and children." Nope, these sins begin with a flirt of

temptation, giving in to the flesh that wants to sabotage you into making unwise decisions that at the moment appear to not be a big deal. We must stay sharp, vigilant, and on point as we daily consider whether each choice we make and action we take is moving us toward or away from our (godly) life creed we established. Scripture is loaded with good advice to count the cost (Luke 14:28) and to consider what we are reaping and sowing (Galatians 6:8; 2 For. 9:6; Proverbs 11:18) and what it means to pay the price (Psalm 126:5; Proverbs 13:21).

3. Acknowledge Your Competitors: This is a race unlike any you have ever competed in as your competition is not against other people but against the world, the flesh, and the devil. How you battle against these will largely determine whether you will finish strong or not. To keep the idea of Coram Deo before you daily will assist you in being able to defeat and be victorious over these competitors that not only want to defeat you but want to see you drop out of the race and completely walk off the track. Stand to and be strong and courageous against these attacks!

4. Keep Eyes Forward: We have examples in Scripture where looking back has not been good. Lot's wife, who wanted to take a look over her shoulder at burning Sodom and Gomorrah, turned into a pillar of salt. Jesus said in Luke 9:62, "No one who puts a hand to the plow and looks back is fit for service in the kingdom of God" (NIV). The question should be asked, "Why would someone look back, or what causes someone to look back?" We look back when something has caught our attention and been a distraction to us. To look back is to lose focus on where we are going. We look back when we don't trust the path and we want to make sure we should keep going forward. In 2017, I recall watching our girls' high school 4x100 team in the state championship final. Immediately it was clear we were one of the top two teams as we were stride for stride with the other teams' girls. As we both simultaneously made our way to the third and final baton hand-off, something

different occurred between our runners and the other top leading girls passing the baton. When their girl was receiving the baton, she turned around to see the runner and the baton being placed in her hand. Conversely, our runner who was waiting with her arm stretched backward and her hand open for the baton to be placed into her hand kept her eyes fixed on the finish line and never once even glanced sideways. The race was won and lost in that very moment. In fact, I slowed down the tape to see it, but there it was, our girl pulled away at that moment, marked by focus for us and uncertainty for the other team as the other girl hesitated for just a moment as she had to reorient her focus that she had lost as she looked over her shoulder. Our team was able to, as Paul says in Philippians 3:14, "Press on toward the goal to win the prize ..." (NIV) as each girl kept their gaze forward. When I consider not just this amazing race but the race of the Christian life, I am reminded of the words in Hebrews that says, "Therefore, since we are surrounded by so great a cloud of witnesses, let us also lay aside every weight, and sin which clings so closely, and let us run with endurance the race that is set before us, looking to Jesus the founder and perfecter of our faith, who for the joy that was set before him endured the cross, despising the shame, and is seated at the right hand of the throne of God (Hebrews 12:1 NIV). Jesus was the perfect model of what it means to be a finisher and to finish strong as Hebrews clearly lays out!

5. Make a Big Push: The same girls who had won the 4x100 were also competing for the 4x400 for the 5A state championship. We knew the other team had some strong runners who were absolutely spectacular, and yet we had four exceptional runners of our own. As the race got underway, it appeared we were not really in the running for the top finish as their lead runner bolted from the starting blocks. By the second hand-off, the other team was twenty-five yards ahead, and by the start of the third hand-off, their lead had grown to around

seventy yards. For a 4x400 race, that gap was just too big to overcome. However, a second place in the state finals is not a bad finish at all—at least that is what observers started to think. But wait, our team was not done! Suddenly when our third runner took the baton, she began to track down their third runner in one of the most amazing athletic feats I have ever seen. Sure, it was physical, but she had to also mentally beat back the thought of quitting and just giving up. Coming into the final turn of the third lap, our third runner took the lead and handed off the baton to our final runner, who flew around that last lap to finish in first place with a state championship team time of 4:05:56! They had prepared and run to finish well by making a big push down the stretch. In fact, it was such a great big push that everyone who saw it was shocked! In the same way, so must we as long as we have breath in our lungs. We should consider how we might finish strong with a good push toward the end, where we are able to do as Paul challenges in 1 Corinthians 9:24, "Do you not know that in a race all the runners run, but only one receives the prize? So run that you may obtain it" (ESV).

As we run and seek to finish strong the race set before us, the writer of Hebrews in 10:36–39 offers us an exhortation, a challenge, and a promise worth hearing,

> You need to persevere so that when you have done the will of God, you will receive what he has promised. For, in just a little while, "He who is coming will come and will not delay. But my righteous one will live by faith. And if he shrinks back, I will not be pleased with him." But we are not of those who shrink back and are destroyed, but of those who believe and are saved. (NIV)

There is no need to be well-rested when attempting to avoid difficult moments, but we need to be courageous to the end, for when we get to heaven, we should be well spent up for the kingdom of God as we finish strong! So right to the end – STAND TO!

Courage Challenge

Very few of us know when the Lord has appointed for us to pass from this life to the next. However, imagine for a moment that you knew when your last month to live was going to be. During that month, the talents you have been blessed with were still in your wheelhouse to be able to execute and your health and energy was good. Consider and then write out how you would spend that last month so as to finish strong, ensuring you were making an eternal significance with the remaining month the Lord had given to you. As you think, let me share one example with you that might both encourage and bring this matter to focus.

Adolphe Monod (1802–1856) was a French preacher that was struck with liver cancer toward the end of his life. Despite being in significant pain, Adolph delivered for the last six months sermons from his bed as his small congregation gathered around him. He spoke of peace, powerful living, joy, living with an eternal perspective, and ultimately his hope of glory. Today we have these twenty-five short sermons in the book called *Living in the Hope of Glory*.

As you plan out your last month on earth, consider these questions and thoughts:

1. Is this something that you can and should be doing right now?
2. Is there is a consistency between what you are now doing and hope to be doing as your life is drawing to a close? In other words, will the trajectory of your life naturally get you to where you would like to end up? (Recall how one degree can really take you away from the target.)

3. If what you have written for your last month is worth doing, then consider if it is worth doing right now! Seriously! Remember, finishing strong does not happen by accident; start now because you never know when you might be living in your last month and not even know it. This is not the time to stand down. It's time to STAND TO!

Appendix 1: Creeds

Air Force, *Airman's Creed*

I am an American Airman.
I am a Warrior.
I have answered my Nation's call.
I am an American Airman.
My mission is to Fly, Fight, and Win.
I am faithful to a Proud Heritage,
A Tradition of Honor,
And a Legacy of Valor.
I am an American Airman.
Guardian of Freedom and Justice,
My Nation's Sword and Shield,
Its Sentry and Avenger.
I defend my Country with my Life.
I am an American Airman.
Wingman, Leader, Warrior.
I will never leave an Airman behind,
I will never falter,
And I will not fail.[108]

Coast Guard, *Creed of the United States Coast Guardsman*

I am proud to be a United States Coast Guardsman.
I revere that long line of expert seamen who by their
devotion to duty and sacrifice of self have made it
possible for me to be a member of a service honored and
respected, in peace and in war, throughout the world.
I never, by word or deed, will bring reproach upon the fair
name of my service, nor permit others to do so unchallenged.
I will cheerfully and willingly obey all lawful orders.
I will always be on time to relieve, and shall endeavor
to do more, rather than less, than my share.
I will always be at my station, alert and attending to my duties.
I shall, so far as I am able, bring to my
seniors solutions, not problems.
I shall live joyously, but always with due regard
for the rights and privileges of others.
I shall endeavor to be a model citizen in
the community in which I live.
I shall sell life dearly to an enemy of my country,
but give it freely to rescue those in peril.
With God's help, I shall endeavor to be
one of His noblest Works …[109]

Marine Corps, *My Rifle—The Creed of a United States Marine*

1. This is my rifle. There are many like it, but this one is mine.
2. My rifle is my best friend. It is my life. I must master it as I must master my life.
3. My rifle, without me, is useless. Without my rifle, I am useless. I must fire my rifle true. I must shoot straighter than my enemy who is trying to kill me. I must shoot him before he shoots me. I will.
4. My rifle and myself know that what counts in this war is not the rounds we fire, the noise of our burst, nor the smoke we make. We know that it is the hits that count. We will hit.
5. My rifle is human, even as I, because it is my life. Thus, I will learn it as a brother. I will learn its weaknesses, its strength, its parts, its accessories, its sights and its barrel. I will ever guard it against the ravages of weather and damage as I will ever guard my legs, my arms, my eyes and my heart against damage. I will keep my rifle clean and ready. We will become part of each other. We will.
6. Before God, I swear this creed. My rifle and myself are the defenders of my country. We are the masters of our enemy. We are the saviors of my life.
7. So be it, until victory is America's and there is no enemy, but peace!![110]

Ranger Creed

Recognizing that I volunteered as a ranger, fully knowing the hazards of my chosen profession, I will always endeavor to uphold the prestige, honor, and high esprit de corps of my ranger regiment. Acknowledging the fact that a ranger is a more elite soldier, who arrives at the cutting edge of battle by land, sea, or air, I accept the fact that as a ranger, my country expects me to move further, faster, and fight harder than any other soldier. Never shall I fail my comrades. I will always keep myself mentally alert, physically strong, and morally straight, and I will shoulder more than my share of the task, whatever it may be, one hundred percent and then some. Gallantly will I show the world that I am a specially selected and well trained soldier. My courtesy to superior officers, neatness of dress, and care of equipment shall set the example for others to follow. Energetically will I meet the enemies of my country. I shall defeat them on the field of battle for I am better trained and will fight with all my might. Surrender is not a ranger word. I will never leave a fallen comrade to fall into the hands of the enemy and under no circumstances will I ever embarrass my country. Readily will I display the intestinal fortitude required to fight on to the ranger objective and complete the mission, though I be the lone survivor.[111]

Navy, *The Sailors' Creed*

I am a United States Sailor.
I will support and defend the Constitution of the United States of
America and I will obey the orders of those appointed over me.
I represent the fighting spirit of the Navy and those who have gone
before me to defend freedom and democracy around the world.
I proudly serve my country's Navy combat team
with Honor, Courage and Commitment.
I am committed to excellence and the fair treatment of all.[112]

ENDNOTES

1 *Dictionary.com,* s.v. "adultescent," accessed November 20, 2020, https://www. dictionary.com/browse/adultescent.

2 Bari Weiss, "Camille Paglia: A Feminist Defense of Masculine Virtues," *Wall Street Journal,* December 28, 2013, https://www.wsj.com/articles/a-feminist-defense-of-masculine-virtuesa-feminist-defense-of-masculine-virtues-1388181961.

3 Jonathan Shieber, "Video game revenue tops $43 billion in 2018, an 18% jump from 2017," *TechCrunch,* January 22, 2019, https://techcrunch.com/2019/01/22/video-game-revenue-tops-43-billion-in-2018-an-18-jump-from-2017/.

4 Kyle Smith, "We're losing a whole generation of young men to video games," *New York Post,* July 8, 2017, https://nypost.com/2017/07/08/were-losing-a-whole-generation-of-young-men-to-video-games/.

5 Kevin Anderton, "Research Report Shows How Much Time We Spend Gaming," *Forbes,* March 21, 2019, https://www.forbes.com/sites/kevinanderton/2019/03/21/research-report-shows-how-much-time-we-spend-gaming-infographic/.

6 "Pornography Statistics," *Covenant Eyes,* accessed November 20, 2020, https://www.covenanteyes.com/pornstats/.

7 "20 Mind-Blowing Stats About The Porn Industry and Its Underage Consumer," Fight the New Drug, May 19, 2020, https://fightthenewdrug.org/10-porn-stats-that-will-blow-your-mind.

8 "Pornography Statistics," *Covenant Eyes,* accessed November 20, 2020, https://www.covenanteyes.com/pornstats/.

9 "Can You Guess 2018's Most-Viewed Categories on the Largest Porn Site?" *Fight the New Drug,* July 9, 2019, https://fightthenewdrug.org/pornhub-visitors-in-2018-and-review-of-top-searches/.

10 Christopher Ingraham, "30-something and still living at home? You've got lots (and lots) of company," *The Washington Post,* May 23, 2018, https://www.washingtonpost.com/news/wonk/wp/2018/05/23/30-something-and-still-living-at-home-youve-got-lots-and-lots-of-company/.

11 Roberto Rivera and John Stonestreet, "Supreme Court Re-Writes 1964 Civil Rights Act: Title VII to Include Sexual Orientation," *Christian Headlines,* June 16, 2020, https://www.christianheadlines.com/columnists/breakpoint/supreme-court-re-writes-1964-civil-rights-act-title-vii-to-include-sexual-orientation.html.

12 David Brooks, *The Social Animal: The Hidden Sources of Love, Character and Achievement* (New York: Random House, 2012), 22.

13 Andrew Murray, *Humility: The Journey Toward Holiness* (Minneapolis: Bethany House, 2001), 45.

14 "Drew Brees: 'Completely missed the mark' in comments on the flag," *ESPN,* June 4, 2020, https://www.espn.com/nfl/story/_/id/29265750/drew-brees-completely-missed-mark-comments-flag.

15 Brett Martel, "Saints quarterback Drew Brees says he still will stand for the national anthem but respect those who kneel," *Sun-Sentinel*, August 1, 2020, https://www.sun-sentinel.com/sports/national-sports/ct-drew-brees-national-anthem-20200801-7cwl34mszfc23bm7bby74fzocm-story.html.

16 Erik Raymond, "The Path to Humility," *The Gospel Coalition,* October 19, 2015, https://www.thegospelcoalition.org/blogs/erik-raymond/the-path-to-humility/.

17 John Dickson, *Humilitas* (Grand Rapids: Zondervan, 2011), 107.

18 Dickson, *Humilitas,* 109.

19 Richard E. Simmons III, *The True Measure of a Man: How Perceptions of Success, Achievement, and Recognition Fail Men in Difficult Times* (Mobile: Genesis Communications Inc., 2013), 97.

20 C. S. Lewis, *Mere Christianity: An Anniversary Edition of the Three Books: The Case for Christianity, Christian Behavior, and Beyond Personality* (New York: Macmillan Publishing Co., Inc., 1952), 102.

21 Nate Pyle, *Man Enough: How Jesus Redefined Manhood* (Grand Rapid: Zondervan Publishing House, 2015), 103.

22 Pyle, *Man Enough,* p.103.

23 Justin Taylor, "Gospel Humility," *The Gospel Coalition,* September 1, 2009, https://www.thegospelcoalition.org/blogs/justin-taylor/gospel-humility/.

24 Jocko Willink and Leif Babin, *Extreme Ownership* (New York: St. Martin's Press, 2015), 27–28.

25 Tim Keller, "Gospel-Humility, *Daily Keller—Wisdom from Tim Keller 365 Days a Year,* February 25, 2015, http://dailykeller.com/gospel-humility/.

26 Paul David Tripp, *Broken-Down House: Living Productively in a World Gone Bad* (Wapwallopen: Shepherd Press, 2009), 17–18.

27 Tripp, *Broken-Down House,* 10.

28 Eric Mason, *Manhood Restored: How the Gospel Makes Men Whole* (Nashville: B&H Publishing Group, 2013), 44.

29 John Eldredge, *Wild at Heart: Discovering the Secret of a Man's Soul* (Nashville: Thomas Nelson, 2001), 122.

30 Larry Crabb, *The Silence of Adam: Becoming Men of Courage in a World of Chaos* (Grand Rapids: Zondervan Publishing House, 1995), 106.

31 Bruce Milne, *The Message of John*, BST, ed. John R.W. Stott (Illinois-Intervarsity Press, 1993), 164.

32 J. Oswald Sanders, *Spiritual Leadership: Principles of Excellence for Every Believer* (Chicago: Moody Publishers, 2007).

33 J.D. Greear, "The Gospel Gives Both Humility and Confidence," *J.D. Greear Ministries,* February 19, 2013, https://jdgreear.com/blog/the-gospel-gives-both-humility-and-confidence/.

34 "C.S. Lewis Quotes," *Goodreads,* accessed November 20, 2020, https://www.goodreads.com/quotes/37169-courage-is-not-simply-one-of-the-virtues-but-the#:~:text=%E2%80%9CCourage%20is%20not%20simply%20one%20of%20the%20virtues%20but%20the,the%20point%20of%20highest%20reality.%20%E2%80%9D.

35 Goodreads, "C.S. Lewis Quotes."

36 Scott Rubarth, "Competing Constructions of Masculinity in Ancient Greece," *Athens Journal of Humanities & Arts* 1 (1)(January 2014): 24.

37 Nicole Johnson, "The Depressing Depiction of Men in the Media," *The Good Men Project,* December 13, 2011, https://goodmenproject.com/featured-content/the-depressing-depiction-of-men-in-the-media/.

38 As quoted by Henderson, *Stonewall Jackson and the American Civil War, vol.1,* 200.

39 Jeff Eisenberg, "The improbably story of how the trendiest chant in sports began," *Yahoo!sports,* June 19, 2014, http://sports.yahoo.com/blogs/soccer-dirty-tackle/the-improbable-story-of-how-the-trendiest-chant-in-sports-began-040228934.html.

40 "Military Creeds at a Glance," *Military.com,* accessed November 20, 2020, http://m.military.com/join-armed-forces/military-creeds.html.

41 David Vergun, "Wounded Warrior Creed Born Out of Suffering," *U.S. Army,* May 13, 2013, http://www.army.mil/article/103134/Wounded_Warrior_Creed_born_out_of_suffering/.

42 Steven R. Watt, "One Warrior's Creed," *Warrior Creed,* accessed November 20, 2020, http://www.warriorcreed.us/.

43 Brett and Kate McKay, "Men Without Chests," *The Art of Manliness,* September 30, 2020, https://www.artofmanliness.com/articles/men-without-chests/.

44 Watt, "One Warrior's Creed."

45 William Tyler Page, "The American's Creed," *UShistory.org,* http://www.ushistory.org/documents/creed.htm.

46 As quoted by Henderson, *Stonewall Jackson and the American Civil War, vol.1*, 200.

47 Mary Thompson, "Ask Mount Vernon," *George Washington's Mount Vernon*, accessed November 20, 2020, https://www.mountvernon.org/the-estate-gardens/ask/question/i-heard-a-story-about-how-george-washington-wore-a-coat-into-battle-and-discovered-afterward-that-the-coat-had-bullet-holes-in-it-can-i-learn-more-about-the-story.

48 R.C. Sproul, "What is a Creed? Christianity Beliefs and History," *Christianity. com*, April 28, 2010, https://www.christianity.com/jesus/early-church-history/early-churches/what-is-a-creed.html.

49 Sproul, "What is a Creed?"

50 William Gurnall, *A Christian in Complete Armour, or, A Treatise of the Saints' War Against the Devil, Wherein a Discovery Is Made of That Grand Enemy of God and His People, in His Policies, Power, Sear of His Empire,* Wickedness, *and Chief Design He Hath Against the Saints* (London: Richard Baynes, 1821), 20.

51 Nicholas Wolterstorff, *Lament for a Son* (Grand Rapid: Wm. B. Eerdmans Publishing Company, 2001), 69.

52 Paul Tautges, "Counseled by the Puritans," *Counseling One Another*, May 29, 2013, https://counselingoneanother.com/2013/05/29/counseled-by-the-puritans-on-providence/.

53 Tautges, "Counseled."

54 James Baumlin and Phillip Sipiora, *Rhetoric and Karios: Essays in History, Theory and Praxis* (Albany: State University of New York Press), 175.

55 Gurnall, *Complete Armour*, 20.

56 Wolterstorff, *Lament*, 70.

57 John McDougall, *Jesus Was an Airborne Ranger* (Colorado Springs: Multnomah Books), 8.

58 Wolterstorff, *Lament*, 81.

59 Wolterstorff, *Lament*, 80.

60 John Henry Jowett, *Streams in the Desert* (Grand Rapids: Zondervan, 1997), 98.

61 Gurnall, *Complete Armour,* 125.

62 Dan Allender, *Leading with a Limp* (Colorado Springs: Waterbrook Press, 2011), 54–55.

63 Marianne Williamson, *Return to Love: Reflections on the Principles of a Course in Miracles* (New York: HarperCollins, 1992), 165.

64 Darren Poke, "The Young Buffalo – A Story About Facing Your Fears," *Better Life Coaching*, March 22, 2013, https://betterlifecoachingblog.com/2013/03/22/the-young-buffalo-a-story-about-facing-your-fears/.

65 Talal Husseini, "Strongest militaries in 2019: comparing global armed forces," *Army Technology,* May 15, 2019, https://www.army-technology.com/features/strongest-militaries-in-2019/.

66 Gurnall, *Complete Armour,* 18.

67 Larry Crabb, "Until a Man is Humbled," *New Way Ministries,* April 9, 2014, https://newwaymin.wordpress.com/2014/04/09/until-a-man-is-humbled/.

68 Williamson, *Return,* 165.

69 "Theodore Roosevelt Quotes," *Goodreads,* accessed November 20, 2020, https://www.goodreads.com/quotes/7-it-is-not-the-critic-who-counts-not-the-man.

70 *Quote Catalog,* accessed November 20, 2020, https://quotecatalog.com/quote/theodore-roosevelt-a-soft-easy-li-L1NO0E7/.

71 Dietrich Bonhoeffer, *Life Together* (New York: HarperCollins, 1954), 115.

72 Bonhoeffer, *Life Together,* 99–100.

73 "Harry Truman Quotes," *Goodreads,* accessed November 20, 2020, https://www.goodreads.com/author/quotes/203941.Harry_Truman.

74 "Being a Man Saying Old Quotes," *Wise Old Sayings,* accessed November 20, 2020, http://www.wiseoldsayings.com/being-a-man-quotes/.

75 Shawn Brower, *We Became Men: The Journey into Manhood* (Phillipsburg: P&R Publishing, 2012), 66.

76 Fatemah Yarali, "9 Inspiring Nelson Mandela Quotes on Forgiveness," *Borgen Porject,* September 30, 2019, https://borgenproject.org/nelson-mandela-quotes-on-forgiveness/.

77 Yarali. "Mandela Quotes."

78 Terez Paylor, "The NFL tried to fine the Saints' Demario Davis for his 'Man of God' headband," *Yahoo Sports,* December 6, 2019, https://sports.yahoo.com/the-nfl-tried-to-fine-the-saints-demario-davis-for-his-man-of-god-headband-heres-what-happened-next-055510651.html.

79 Paylor, "Demario Davis."

80 "Charles R. Swindoll Quotes," *Goodreads,* accessed November 20, 2020, https://www.goodreads.com/quotes/829722-this-is-a-story-about-four-people-named-everybody-somebody.

81 "The Competitor's Creed," *Fellowship of Christian Athletes, accessed November 20, 2020,* http://fcaendurance.org/resources.

82 "Give Me Liberty Or Give Me Death!" *Colonial Williamsburg,* March 3, 2020, https://colonialwilliamsburg.org/learn/deep-dives/give-me-liberty-or-give-me-death/.

83 Jaffer Ali, "Secret of Victory—By George S. Patton with Commentary by Jaffer Ali," *Jaffer Ali,* May 14, 2017, https://medium.com/@jafferali1956/secret-of-victory-by-george-s-patton-with-commentary-by-jaffer-ali-574aa96b172e.

84 "Gaylord Nelson Quotes," *Goodreads, accessed November 20, 2020,* https://www.goodreads.com/author/quotes/145890.Gaylord_Nelson.

85 A. Guttmann, "Advertising Spending in the U.S. 2015-2022," *Statista,* March 28, 2019, https://www.statista.com/statistics/272314/advertising-spending-in-the-us/.

86 Marjorie Jackson, "He Makes Us Strong," *Marjorie Jackson,* Wordpress, March 14, 2016, https://marjoriejackson.wordpress.com/2016/03/14/he-makes-us-strong/.

87 Rachel Greenspan, "Here Are the Highest-Grossing Marvel Movies," *Time,* July 21, 2019, https://time.com/5523398/highest-grossing-marvel-movies/.

88 "List of Marvel Cinematic Universal Films," *Wikipedia,* accessed November 20, 2020, https://en.m.wikipedia.org/wiki/List_of_Marvel_Cinematic_Universe_films.

89 Allender, *Limp,* 55.

90 Allender, *Limp,* 56.

91 Wayne Cordeiro, *Leading on Empty* (Grand Rapids: Baker Publishing House, 2009), 69.

92 Cordeiro, *Empty,* 69.

93 Cordeiro, *Empty,* 48.

94 Cordeiro, *Empty,* 76–77.

95 Nathan Bingham, "Justification by Faith Alone: Martin Luther and Romans 1:7," *Ligonier Ministries,* October 6, 2019, https://www.ligonier.org/blog/justification-faith-alone-martin-luther-and-romans-117/.

96 Dan Graves, "Here I stand, I can do no other, so help me God. Amen." *Christian History Institute,* October 20, 2016, https://christianhistoryinstitute.org/blog/post/here-i-stand-i-can-do-no-other/.

97 Goodreads, "Dorothy Sayers Quotes."

98 Travis Bradberry, "Why the Best Leaders Have Conviction," *Forbes,* June 28, 2016, https://www.forbes.com/sites/travisbradberry/2016/06/28/why-the-best-leaders-have-conviction/#322d6ddc1c8d.

99 Albert Mohler, "Leading with Conviction," *Tabletalk,* November 2017, https://tabletalkmagazine.com/article/2017/11/leading-with-conviction/.

100 Mohler, "Conviction."

101 C. S. Lewis, *The Screwtape Letters* (New York: McMillian Company, 1943) 64.

102 Peter Greer and Chris Horst, *Mission Drift: The Unspoken Crisis Facing Leaders, Charities, and Churches*
(Bloomington: Bethany House Publishers, 2014), 92.

103 Arnold Cook, *Historical Drift: Must My Church Die?* (Chicago, Moody Publisher, 2008), 164.

104 "Bishops Ridley and Latimer Burned," *Christianity.com. May 3, 2010,* https://www.christianity.com/church/church-history/timeline/1501-1600/bishops-ridley-and-latimer-burned-11629990.html.

105 Stephen E. Ambrose, *Band of Brothers* (New York: Simon & Schuster, 1992), 293.

106 Ambrose, *Brothers,* 293.

107 "Mindset Story: The Greatest Last Place," *Purpose, Focus, Commitment,* accessed November 20, 2020, https://purposefocuscommitment.com/the-greatest-last-place-ever/.

108 "Military Creeds at a Glance," Military.com, *accessed November 20, 2020,* http://m.military.com/join-armed-forces/military-creeds.html.

109 Militarycreeds.com, "Military Creeds."

110 Militarycreeds.com, "Military Creeds."

111 Militarycreeds.com, "Military Creeds."

112 Militarycreeds.com, "Military Creeds."

Also Available from

SHAWN BROWER

Printed in the United States
By Bookmasters